Mowgli and the animals of **The Jungle Book** *are probably Kipling's most famous and best-loved characters. In 1965 Walt Disney produced a cartoon film based on the book which was a tremendous box-office success and also delighted the critics. Here are Mowgli and the other "stars" of the film.*

Giants of Literature

Kipling

Sampson Low

Contents

''I had always been choice . . . . . .''   5

The Anglo-Indian Empire   6

The Life of Kipling   9

Kipling the Man   25

The Works of Kipling   33

The Art of the Punjab   49

A Kipling Anthology   57

Kipling's Characters   89

The World of Kim   105

The British in India   113

Kipling and the Critics   121

Editions of Kipling's Works   135

© 1968 Arnoldo Mondadori Editore, Milan

English Language Edition first published in 1977 by Sampson Low,

Berkshire House, Queen Street, Maidenhead, Berkshire, England.

Printed and bound in Italy by Arnoldo Mondadori Editore.

"I had always been choice . . ."

"And with what tools did I work in my own mould-loft? I had always been choice, not to say coquettish in this respect. In Lahore for my *Plain Tales* I used a slim, octagonal-sided, agate penholder with a Waverley nib. It was a gift, and when in an evil hour it snapped I was much disturbed. Then followed a procession of impersonal hirelings each with a Waverley, and next a silver penholder with a quill-like curve, which promised well but did not perform. In Villiers Street I got me an outsize office pewter ink-pot, on which I would gouge the names of the tales and books I wrote out of it. But the housemaids of married life polished those titles away till they grew as faded as a palimpsest.

"I then abandoned hand-dipped Waverleys – a nib I never changed – and for years wallowed in the pin-pointed 'stylo' and its successor the 'fountain' which for me meant geyser-pens. In later years I clung to a slim, smooth, black treasure (Jael was her office name) which I picked up in Jerusalem. I tried pump-pens with glass insides, but they were of 'intolerable entrails'.

"For my ink I demanded the blackest, and had I been in my Father's house, as once I was, would have kept an ink-boy to grind me an Indian-ink. All 'blue-blacks' were an abomination to my Daemon, and I never found a bottled vermilion fit to rubricate initials when one hung in the wind waiting.

"My writing-blocks were built for me to an unchanged pattern of large, off-white, blue sheets, of which I was most wasteful. All this old-maiderie did not prevent me when abroad from buying and using blocks, and tackle, in any country.

"With a lead pencil I ceased to express – probably because I had to use a pencil in reporting. I took very few notes except of names, dates, and addresses. If a thing didn't stay in my memory, I argued it was hardly worth writing out. But each man has his method. I rudely drew what I wanted to remember.

"Like most men who ply one trade in one place for any while, I always kept certain gadgets on my work-table, which was ten feet long from North to South and badly congested. One was a long, lacquer, canoe-shaped pen-tray full of brushes and dead 'fountains'; a wooden box held clips and bands; another, a tin one, pins; yet another, a bottle-slider, kept all manner of unneeded essentials from emery-paper to small screwdrivers; a paper-weight, said to have been Warren Hastings'; a tiny, weighted fur-seal and a leather crocodile sat on some of the papers; an inky foot-rule and a Father of Penwipers which a much-loved housemaid of ours presented yearly, made up the main-guard of these little fetishes.

"My treatment of books, which I looked upon as tools of my trade, was popularly regarded as barbarian. Yet I economised on my multitudinous penknives, and it did no harm to my forefinger. There were books which I respected, because they were put in locked cases. The others, all the house over, took their chances.

"Left and right of the table were two big globes, on one of which a great airman had once outlined in white paint those air-routes to the East and Australia which were well in use before my death."

Rudyard Kipling

From *Something of Myself, for my Friends Known and Unknown.*

5

The Anglo-Indian Empire

In 1865, when Rudyard Kipling was born in Bombay, the political unification of India under British rule was a *fait accompli* and the country was gradually taking on the guise of a modern state. Over two centuries had elapsed since the Great Mogul of Agra, Jahangir, had first authorised the English East India Company to establish fortified trading posts on the Indian peninsula and to govern the land according to British law. For many years the Company (essentially a trading organisation set up and run by the British government) devoted itself exclusively to commercial activities but towards the middle of the 18th century the progressive dismemberment of the Mogul Empire and the need to counter the threat of the rival French East India Company forced it to adopt a genuine policy of colonial expansion, so that in due course it acquired sovereignty over an even larger area of the subcontinent. From 1774 until 1849 a series of wars against the French, as well as against local national groups – especially the Marathas – extended British occupation and rule over a territory inhabited by about 200 million people.

The British parliament, at first opposed to expansionist adventures, eventually claimed for itself the right to administer the conquered regions. As a result of a series of Regulating Acts the Company (which ceased to exist in 1858) saw itself substantially deprived of executive power which finally passed into the hands of a governor general who com-

manded the armed forces and was appointed by the Crown. The official policy of non-interference with local administration and customs, strictly enforced in the early years, was opposed at home by a powerful coalition of evangelists and utilitarians who claimed that the British government was duty bound to introduce sweeping reforms in India, designed to encourage moral progress and social advancement. Also in favour of such reforms was a group of Hindu intellectuals whose leader and spokesman was Ram Mohan Roy (1772–1833), a liberal-minded Brahmin. Ram Mohan Roy also led the fight for the teaching of English instead of native dialects in secondary schools. He realised that a language that was common to the entire population, even if that of a foreign occupying power, could be the starting point for the formation of a movement inspired by the ideal of national independence.

The India where Rudyard Kipling spent his childhood and much of his youth, and where he first embarked on the journalistic career that was to introduce him to the world of literature, was the "new India" that had evolved slowly and painfully over a period of two hundred years. It was a country of fascinating contrasts and contradictions which, in accordance with the complex rules of national self interest, had steadily been developed – and exploited – by its colonial rulers. Among the more positive aspects of the British administration at that time were

an impressive building programme designed to improve road, railway and telegraphic communications, the adoption of modern agricultural methods and the introduction of various reforms in the legal and financial spheres. Less laudable was the serious blow to the nation's economy caused by the catastrophic ruin of the local textile industry – unable to compete with the mass-produced articles turned out by English factories. Crowds of unemployed roamed the countryside, aggravating an already alarming over-population problem in rural areas and provoking an ever-increasing flow of emigration to the British colonies in Africa and Australasia, and to the United States.

The village remained the corner-stone of Indian economic and social life but the pattern of rural existence was virtually untouched by progress, hampered by seemingly unbreakable links with the past. Tyrannous absentee landlords were still entitled to impose an outrageous rate of annual taxation of up to 75 per cent, and agricultural production was severely curtailed as a result of wasteful religious rites and customs. At the same time, however, Madras, Bombay, Lahore and Calcutta were being transformed into modern cities – seats of the first Indian universities. "Pax Britannica" resulted in India being politically isolated from the rest of the world but the increasingly widespread circulation of newspapers and journals was creating an ever-larger network of communications among people of many

A battle between the Sikhs and the British, a wood-engraving from John Lockwood Kipling's collection (1870).

different races and backgrounds. This was to prove a powerful force in the gradual emergence of a national consciousness. So it was that the legendary image of "Mother India" took shape – an image that was nurtured by pamphlets and newspaper articles dealing with the ethnic and social problems of the indigenous population.

With the slow decline of native culture and the gradual breakdown of the caste system there emerged in the cities an intellectual middle class, no longer restricted by local taboos, which chose to adopt the life style of the British raj. These people read Shakespeare, Dickens and Thackeray, played cricket, polo and hockey, attended garden parties and took afternoon tea. Far more important than these superficial attitudes and habits, however, was the influence of western ideas – the discovery of the principles of democracy, equality, individual worth and personal freedom – which made a revolutionary impact on the Indian mind.

The new middle class expanded, swelled by graduates from the universities, so that in time it acquired an individual quality, being composed of people whom the historian and politician Macaulay described as Indians in blood and skin colour but English in tastes, opinions, morality and intelligence. In the forefront of this newly evolved social class were the lawyers – direct intermediaries between the government and the people – from whose ranks eventually emerged leaders of the national independence movement such as Gandhi and Nehru.

It was therefore inevitable that these westernised Indians should be the first to cherish hopes, however vague and confused, of independence as a natural reaction against the moral and economic pressures of foreign rule. Although it never took as extreme a form as in the African colonies, there was a deliberate policy of racial discrimination in India which was manifested in various ways. Thus Indians were still virtu-

ally excluded from politics, despite a few cautious local administrative reforms introduced in the last two decades of the 19th century after Queen Victoria adopted the title of Empress of India. Indians were also very heavily taxed in order to contribute to the expenses of the army and civil service, a vast bureaucratic machine made up of British officials.

In 1885 the middle classes, largely represented by groups of professional men, found their own mouthpiece in the first Indian National Congress, formed as a semi-political association which professed its staunch loyalty to the British Crown and for twenty years was content to sit back and wait hopefully for Britain to provide the necessary impetus towards national progress and prosperity. But at the beginning of the 20th century the strengthening of the middle classes and the emergence of an industrial working class encouraged the Congress to undertake a radical revision of its objectives and plans. Political action now assumed increasing importance, the main and over-riding aim being to obtain the right of self-government within the British Empire, and then to work for complete independence. The revitalised Congress, rich in talents, was soon to become the one real symbol of the new India – an India that aspired to self-rule yet was not prepared to turn the clock back or to destroy the elaborate social, economic and political system created by the British.

The Life of Kipling

As an Englishman born and bred in India, land of fable and mystery, Kipling imbibed ideas and gathered themes for a lifetime of literary activity.

A wondrous childhood

Joseph Rudyard Kipling was born in Bombay on 30 December 1865. His parents, John Lockwood Kipling and Alice Macdonald, had recently come to India in the hope of making their fortune. Like many of their countrymen who sprang from a well-to-do background but had lately come down in the world because of economic difficulties, they had decided to try their luck in the colonies, convinced that their practical and cultural gifts could be put to better use in a completely new environment. John Kipling was a scholar, art critic and amateur ethnologist, who had been made director of the Bombay School of Art. His wife, related to some of the most famous artists of the Victorian age (including Burne-Jones) was hopeful that she would be able to lead the same kind of life she had so enjoyed in London – cultured drawing-room conversation and all – in India.

Rudyard Kipling's earliest years were comfortable. His parents were in daily contact with the leading lights of Bombay society and their circumstances were steadily improving. He grew up loved, well provided for and without inhibitions, thanks to a liberal home atmosphere and a tolerant and informal system of educa-

Facing page: *Rudyard Kipling in a photograph taken in 1885 at the age of twenty. He had already been hailed as a brilliant and very promising young writer and journalist by the Anglo-Indian community. This was the juncture in his career when he was beginning to publish his first stories.*
Above: *a street in Bombay, the city where Rudyard Kipling was born (painting by W. Carpenter).*

Below: *Rudyard Lake in Scotland, where Kipling's parents John and Alice,* **right,** *first met. They decided to name their son after the place which had a special romantic association for them.*

tion in which there was no need for harsh discipline. The members of Anglo-Indian society were privileged but not necessarily inactive and insensible. Surrounded as they were by such a medley of races and religions, exposed to such a multitude of contrasting ideas and impressions, they tended to have a rather freer, broader outlook on life than most of their middle-class counterparts back home, where attitudes were more conventional and puritanical. The young Rudyard was entrusted to the care of a Roman Catholic *ayah* from Portuguese Goa and a Hindu bearer; and one of his companions was a Parsee friend of his father named Pestonjee Bomonjee. Thus from earliest childhood he became familiar with a wide variety of customs and beliefs, learning to speak local Indian dialects even before English.

His days passed uneventfully in the company of the children of his parents' servants. He possessed boundless energy and delighted in playing noisy games but he also enjoyed sitting quietly listening to the marvellous stories and legends that the natives knew by heart and recounted in such vivid language. Naturally and effortlessly he imbibed the magic of India that was to be the richest source of his literary inspiration. Indeed his only white friend at that time was "Terry Sahib", his father's assistant at the School of Art, who allowed him to play with sculptor's clay in the school's studio.

Rough interlude

Those carefree years of childhood all too soon came to an abrupt end. At the age of six the boy was sent to England to begin his serious schooling. This was fairly common practice among the wealthier Anglo-Indian residents who were anxious for their sons, once

10

At the age of six Rudyard was sent by his parents to school in England. The harsh discipline and unbending morality of his foster-mother Aunty Rosa led him to suffer a nervous breakdown. A welcome respite was provided by his visits to his aunt Georgina, married to the painter Edward Burne-Jones. **Left**: *the dining-room of their house, The Grange (watercolour by Rook).* **Right**: *a photo of the seven-year-old Kipling.*

A writer and art critic, John Lockwood Kipling (seen below in a terracotta relief done by himself) wanted his son to have the best possible education and sent him to the United Services College in Devon, the headmaster of which was a family *friend, Cormell Price* (photograph at bottom of page). *Rudyard received a traditional public-school education based on hard discipline and self-sacrifice. In the photograph he is seen with two of his friends.*

having reached the right age, to receive a proper English education. They deemed it important because a boy's future, if he were to follow in his father's footsteps, depended on his gaining the necessary certificates and awards from an English school or university. The general procedure, if there were no close relatives available, was to board the child privately, perhaps in the house of a respectable elderly couple in some provincial town. In exchange for a modest rent they undertook to keep their charges in reasonably good health and see that they went to a school offering a sound, strict curriculum.

But such arrangements did not invariably have the happiest results. For many a child born abroad in the colonies, those long years of schooling and accommodation with foster-parents proved an endless torment, aggravated by sad memories of their distant families. In some cases the mental suffering was worse than the physical, leaving deep, ineradicable scars.

In 1871 Rudyard and his younger sister Trix arrived at Southsea, near Portsmouth, to attend day school at Hope House, Somerset Place. They were sent to live with Captain and Mrs Holloway, and their twelve-year-old son Harry,

NORTH VIEW OF THE CITY OF LAHORE

who, in Rudyard's eyes, emerged as a kind of sadistic tyrant. Captain Holloway had been in the merchant navy, but long retired, he had lost all trace of any authority he might once have wielded over members of his crew. Now he passed his time on the town quay, looking wistfully at the old ships and taking no interest whatsoever in what went on at home, where his grimly evangelical wife "Aunty Rosa" imposed rigid discipline by means of beatings, inadequate meals and moral lectures, which got worse after her husband's sudden death. The children lived in the Holloway house for six years.

In all that time one of the few comforts for the boy was to read the books that his parents occasionally sent him from India. This was strictly forbidden by Aunty Rosa, so that he was forced to read them secretly, usually at night when the rest of the family were asleep. The practice left him short-sighted at an early age and also led to a nervous breakdown.

Journalism in India

In 1877 Alice Kipling paid a visit to England, alarmed by the news she had received from one of her sisters about her son's poor state of health. She spent several months in London with Rudyard who was by this time too depressed and weak even to attend school. Before leaving the country she found a more suitable establishment for her son who, probably because of the hardships endured at Southsea, seemed more mature than other boys of his age. The United Services College at Westward Ho! in Devon was a boarding school run by Cormell Price, an old family friend. Life at the school was tough (Kipling was to write a short novel, *Stalky & Co*, based on his experiences there) but not unrewarding.

13

Now that he was adolescent he was better equipped to face four more years of separation from his parents; and it was during that period in Devon that he made his first literary experiments – the *Schoolboy Lyrics*, short satirical verses which his mother later collected and had published in India in 1881.

In the meantime, however, the fortunes of the family suffered a setback and his father's dreams of becoming rich vanished for ever. Partly because of this and partly because Rudyard's poor eyesight made it unlikely that he could look forward to a government job,

the decision was made to cut short the boy's education. So instead of going on to an English university he was brought back to India early in 1882, settling in Lahore where his father had managed to get a position as curator of the city museum.

Rudyard's future was soon decided. Mature beyond his sixteen years, capable of making friends easily, he settled down well in the job his father had found for him on the staff of an English paper, *The Civil and Military Gazette*. In the five years he held this post he learned the journalist's trade and became assistant to the

paper's owner-manager. A series of his short stories, published weekly, soon earned him a reputation in the Anglo-Indian community. These delightful stories, full of action and local colour, were collected in 1888 and published as *Plain Tales from the Hills*.

Kipling in due course was offered a better job on the *Pioneer*, the most important English-language daily newspaper in India, printed in Allahabad, administrative capital of the colony. In 1886, a year before he took up his new position, he had brought out his own small volume of verse, the *Departmental Ditties*, his first

Below: *Caroline Balestier, who became Kipling's wife in 1892 (painting by Philip Burne-Jones).*
Right: *a view of Simla, summer capital of the British Raj, in the Himalayas. Simla and its· surroundings were the setting for* Plain Tales from the Hills, *published in 1888. A year later Kipling went on a round-the-world trip for his newspaper the* Pioneer, *and in 1891 arrived in London, where he was expected to send back reports about England.*

work to be published in England.

While working as assistant director of the *Pioneer* Kipling wrote a series of stories that marked his real arrival in the world of letters. They were published by the Railway Library and were sold on the news-stands of railway stations at the price of one rupee each. Soon the name of the new young author was known throughout India and, more significantly, in England and America as well. Just as successful as his stories were his newspaper reports which were far superior to the average journalism of the time. Keeping a close watch on daily events, Kipling produced articles that were lively, informative and thought-provoking. The director of the *Pioneer*, realising that, in racing terms, his assistant was a "pure thoroughbred colt", offered to send him on a trip round the world, ending up in England, in the course of which he would be expected to send back reports to the paper.

In 1889 Kipling sailed for San Francisco and went on to Chicago and New York, arriving in Liverpool in early October. The articles he regularly despatched from these cities were later collected together in a volume called *Letters of*

Marque. Arriving in London he took cheap lodgings in the Strand; but by 1890 his literary acclaim was far in advance of his personal and financial circumstances. His first stories had been received in England with surprise and pleasure, and already some critics were hailing him as a refreshing and significant new voice in the world of letters. The voice was all the more welcome among discerning reviewers for being so pointedly at odds with the current vogue of aesthetic romanticism which had exhausted its springs of inspiration and which appealed only to a closed circle of sympathisers and connoisseurs. Kipling's vigorous style and original subject matter appealed to all classes of reader, even the less educated and cultured. With *Plain Tales from the Hills*, *The Three Musketeers*, *The Phantom Rickshaw* and similar stories, Kipling created a literary genre that had not previously existed in Victorian England and won himself immediate popularity and success.

Prophet of imperialism

During this year in London (1890), Kipling wrote and published his first novel, *The Light that Failed.* It was not a tremendously successful work financially but, by virtue of the discussion it aroused, helped to make his name even better known. The critics accused the young author of using over-violent language and of treating a controversial theme (the love of a war artist for the haughty sweetheart of his childhood) with excessive frankness. Kipling himself was forced to admit, years later, that the book was not one of his happiest. The critical hostility caused such emotional tension that he came perilously close to a recurrence of the alarming form of nervous breakdown he had suffered as

16

a boy. Feeling the urgent need to relax and get away from the heated atmosphere of literary controversy, he set out on a second trip round the world, visiting America, South Africa, Australia and New Zealand. The cruise itinerary took him to other British colonies and first made him aware of what he called the "white man's burden" whereby his many compatriots, often well-meaning, dedicated individuals, worked and often suffered in their efforts to promote the interests of the British government and realise the Imperial dream. It was in the course of this long journey that Kipling first began dimly to perceive his mission as spokesman and prophet of the Imperial ideal, which was to be one of the principal motivating forces of his career, especially as formulated in his verse. Kipling's attitude to the Empire was bitterly attacked, though not properly understood, in his lifetime; and it still arouses keen controversy, preventing many critics from making a thorough and objective assessment of his literary achievement.

In January 1892 Kipling returned to London and soon afterwards married Caroline Walcott Balestier, sister of a dear friend and colleague, Wolcott Balestier, an American publisher, who had recently died.

In 1900, a few months after the outbreak of the Boer War, Kipling left for South Africa as a war correspondent. **Right**: Boer soldiers at the front. **Below**: a painting by Giles of the British cavalry advancing on Kimberley.

It was to be a happy marriage, lasting a lifetime, and from it came three children, two girls and a boy. After the wedding the Kiplings left for a long honeymoon but an unexpected failure of the bank where Rudyard had deposited his first earnings compelled them to remain in the United States, at his wife's home in Vermont. The American interlude lasted four years and was one of the most prolific creative periods of his life. It was here that he wrote the two *Jungle Books* that spread his fame all over the civilised world. By now he was one of the most widely read and discussed authors in America and Europe; and it was while he remained in the United States that he began earning really large amounts of money. Publishers fought for the privilege of bringing out his short stories and the most influential newspapers of the day outbid one another to sign him up as a contributor. He broadened his circle of acquaintances, becoming a friend of Theodore Roosevelt and of such eminent figures of the publishing world as Henry Harper, who had pointedly snubbed him when he had been unknown. His two daughters, Josephine and Elsie, were both born in America.

In August 1897 the Kiplings returned to England and bought a house in the seaside village of Rottingdean where their son John was born. The trips to the United States had given Rudyard the idea for a new novel, *Captains Courageous*. Now a mature writer, he was respected and admired by the public both for his literary achievements and the range of his interests. He eagerly undertook civic responsibilities and began to take an active part in politics, not surprisingly as a supporter of the Conservative party. But he was soon to come up against adverse criticism and outright hostility. Initial enthusiasm for his literary works

Below: *an illustration for Kipling's poem* The Absent-Minded Beggar. *The £250 which he received for this poem was earmarked for a fund for the British troops in South Africa. Kipling was severely critical of official mismanagement which* he blamed for the high casualty rate which was being incurred by the army. His opponents hit back at him with caricatures and satirical articles. Here he is shown in his professional capacity "on the spot".

was gradually overshadowed by disapproval of his public pronouncements, and he was labelled both an "imperialist" and a "warmonger". Actually Kipling's works show many indications of a somewhat confused attitude towards political events. He evidently felt that his popularity carried a heavy weight of responsibility, conferring upon himself a mission that he was duty bound to acknowledge and fulfil as best he could. In 1899 he published his most famous poem, *The White Man's Burden*, in which he extolled the noble, civilising influence of the West. At about that time he stopped writing

stories based on Indian memories and experiences, devoting himself instead to more serious works of a moral and didactic nature. In 1899 he brought out *Stalky & Co*, a collection of anecdotes based on his years at Westward Ho!, the main purpose of which was to paint for a new generation a pretty gloomy picture of the schools and educational methods that had traditionally moulded the English gentleman. It was vehemently attacked by those who were out of sympathy with Kipling's satirical intentions and even more unexpectedly criticised by some of his friends. Two real persons on whom the

characters of M'Turk and Stalky were based – George Beresford and Lionel Dunsterville – later wrote books to refute or correct much of what Kipling had written, entitled respectively *Schooldays with Kipling* and *Stalky's Reminiscences*. The poor reception of *Stalky & Co* saddened Kipling but he did not try to hit back at his critics, accepting that it was the lot of the writer to live on hopes and sometimes to suffer disappointment.

Nobel Prize for Literature

Once again, partly with a view to escaping from a society that

After several years in Rottingdean the Kiplings moved to Burwash in Sussex, where they bought a house, **below**. Their three children, Elsie, John and Josephine are seen in the photograph on the right, taken shortly before Josephine died. John, born in 1897, was killed in the First World War. **Facing page**, **left**: Kim and the Scribe, *a terracotta relief by John Kipling used for an illustration to his son's world acclaimed masterpiece* Kim.

did not sympathise with his own cherished ideals, based on the concept of personal sacrifice and the spirit of adventure, Kipling decided to leave England, this time to become a war correspondent with the British troops sent out to South Africa to fight the Boers. It was a testing experience and in a way sharpened his resolve to look back to a nobler, more purposeful past as the true embodiment of an Imperial ideal that seemed to be losing much of its impetus. He was convinced that the initial embarrassing failure of the British army to defeat the Boers was a warning signal that the great Empire ruled by Queen Victoria (who died in January 1901 while the war was still raging) was doomed to slow decline. Perhaps because of this realisation Kipling once more turned for literary inspiration to the world of his childhood. It was in 1901 that his masterpiece *Kim* was published.

The eventual victory of the British over the Boers re-awakened his old ardour for the Empire; and in the next five years he brought out two works which in their different ways openly celebrated the greatness of Britain – *The Five Nations* (1903) and *Puck of Pook's Hill* (1906). The former was a collection of ballads and poems recording the Boer War experience in characteristically blunt language and strong, simple rhythms. The latter was a collection of stories inspired by British history and legend, intended for children, in which many exciting episodes of the past, from the Roman Conquest to the battles between the Saxons and Normans, were paraded in fictional form.

Rudyard Kipling's great year was 1907 when he was awarded the Nobel Prize for Literature. He was 42 years old, at the height of his fame. But from then onwards both his reputation and popularity started to wane. The award was wel-

21

comed throughout Europe as giving deserved recognition to a writer who was beloved and admired by young and adult readers the world over. Yet, ironically, in England, the news was received coldly; and it was at home too that the first signs of his dwindling reputation appeared. It was dealt a severe blow in 1909 when he came up against Lloyd George, the Welsh politician whose dream was to initiate an ambitious programme of social reform. Kipling was especially disturbed by the demands of the trade unions who were claiming a right to be represented in government. He felt that the attitudes and aims of the unions were detrimental to the true interests of the British working classes which, in his opinion, could best be furthered by their continuing to go about their everyday activities with a proper sense of dedication and responsibility. Although Kipling was strongly opposed to outright exploitation of the workers he had no time for the "crusading" terms in which the Liberal party and radicals in general defended their principles.

In 1914 the outbreak of the First World War took Kipling back to the firing line as a military correspondent, first on the western front and then in Italy. From both theatres of war he sent first-hand reports to the leading English newspapers. Although he had lost some of his old journalistic flair, his articles were written with scrupulous and often angry objectivity. In the first weeks of the war he lost his son John, killed in battle. A selection of his Italian articles was published in book form under the title *War in the Mountains*, including vivid descriptions of the tough campaigns of the Italians against the Austrians in the Alps.

With the return of peace Kipling resumed his tireless literary activity, arranging for new editions and collections of

1 *In 1915, in the early part of the war, Kipling delivers a recruitment speech.* **2** *The writer and his wife in 1920.* **3** *King George V and Kipling at a war cemetery in Belgium.* **4** *The Kiplings on their way to Buckingham Palace.*

his most famous works. His unfinished book, *Something of Myself, for my Friends Known and Unknown*, was written in that period, to be published posthumously in 1937. It is not a real autobiography nor an attempt to justify his political beliefs, but a delightful collection of childhood memories and random reflections from the happier moments of later life. From these pages emerges a revealing self-portrait. The man pictured here is determined, extrovert, hopeful of the future, loyal in affections, generous and ironic in judgment, diligent in everything attempted, whether in private or in public.

Rudyard Kipling died suddenly in London on 18 January 1936. He was given an impressive funeral and even the bitterest opponents of his political opinions were now forced to recognise the prophetic truth of the warnings he had sounded in many of his works. Within another few years another catastrophic world war had erupted. At the end of it, although on the victorious side, Great Britain gradually came to realise that the glowing days of Empire were drawing to a close and that she would now have to assume a more modest role in international affairs – a role which Kipling, had he lived, would probably have been unable to endure.

Kipling the Man

"The frame of mind which he really describes with beauty and nobility is the frame of mind of the cosmopolitan man who has seen men and cities.
For to admire and for to see
For to be'old this world so wide.
He is a perfect master of that light melancholy with which a man looks back on having been the citizen of many communities, of that light melancholy with which a man looks back on having been the lover of many women."

G. K. CHESTERTON

The Diamond Jubilee

Since the fall of the Roman Empire no nation had extended its dominion over such a vast region as Great Britain. British possessions abroad covered more than one-quarter of the earth's land surface. When, on 22 June 1897, the sixtieth anniversary of Queen Victoria's accession to the throne, a magnificent royal procession wound its way through the streets of London, few citizens had any doubts as to the enduring greatness of the Empire. It was significant, however, that not a single foreign head of state was invited to attend the Diamond Jubilee celebrations. Colonial leaders, on the other hand, were well represented. Ceremonial coaches were provided for the eleven prime ministers of Canada, New Zealand, Cape Colony, Natal, Newfoundland and the six Australian states. Colonial military detachments, too, marched with their famous British counterparts – infantry and cavalry regiments, the latter including the Cape Mounted Rifles, the Canadian Hussars, the New South Wales Lancers, the Trinidad Light Cavalry and

Lancers from Khapurthala, Nadnagar and other Indian states, led by officers in white turbans.

It was a glittering spectacle and it undoubtedly warmed the hearts of loyal English men and women for whom the sight of the colourful marching columns symbolised the nation's power. At the end of the procession, in an open carriage drawn by eight white horses, came Queen Victoria, tiny, dressed in black with a small hat adorned with white feathers. She was visibly moved by the sight of the cheering crowds and recorded in her diary that she believed nobody had ever received such an ovation.

Strangely, one of the few voices to sound a slightly sour note on that memorable occasion was that of Rudyard Kipling. On the next day *The Times* published his most austere poem, *Recessional*, a warning to Britain not to try to emulate the arrogance of Tyre and Nineveh. Few people, however, paid much heed to the message which the most famous English writer of the day was trying to convey. The sense of the grandeur and glory of the British Empire was

so deeply rooted that no patriot could imagine it not lasting for ever. Furthermore, since Kipling himself was recognised as the most voluble supporter of the Imperial ideal it hardly became him to start issuing warnings, however gentle, of danger and doom.

Kipling was at that time 32 years old. Many contemporaries had been surprised, and some shocked, at his early ascent up the ladder of fame, but by now he had become the symbol of a political creed and a style of life that inspired pride and confidence. The opinions that he expressed, whether elegantly in the form of newspaper reports from distant lands, or in a more down-to-earth manner in popular ballads and verses, were familiar and comforting. In their different ways both were regarded as justifications for a steady expansion of Imperial power which, to the man in the street, appeared natural, inevitable and indestructible.

Any modern attempt to examine the reasons for Kipling's high reputation in his day, apart from those stemming merely from literary genius, must take account of the environment where he grew up and the civilisation which formed the background of his early life. The key fact is that he was born of English parents who made their home in India shortly after their marriage. His father, John Lockwood Kipling, was a well-read, intelligent man with a wide range of cultural interests. A competent artist, he could converse freely and write convincingly about art criticism, literature, archaeology and ethnology. In 1891 he wrote a book called *Beast and Man in India*, something of a hotchpotch but containing a wealth of observations and lively sketches that were certainly used by his son Rudyard for the *Jungle Books*. His mother, Alice, was also a genuinely cultured person with an openness of mind remarkable for a woman of her time. The friends and acquaintances they had left behind in London included some of the most brilliant talents of the day. Alice's brother-in-law was the painter Edward Burne-Jones (Rudyard knew him as Uncle Ned) and among the distinguished guests at her wedding were Dante Gabriel Rossetti and his sister Christina, Ford Madox Brown and Algernon Swinburne. It is apparent, therefore, that from the very beginning the young Rudyard had the advantage of a family atmosphere in which his own artistic inclinations and gifts could be fostered and cultivated.

Christianity and oriental mysticism

Rudyard Kipling was born in Bombay where his father was director of the Art School. His somewhat unusual name was that of the small lake in Scotland where his parents had first met – a pleasantly romantic touch, conveying something of the intensity of their love for each other, which remained one of Rudyard's happiest childhood memories. It was a love that expressed itself openly throughout their lives, helped forge strong family bonds between boy and parents while separated for many years during adolescence and remained just as firm when he became a famous writer.

The earliest days, therefore, were full of affection and joy. In *Something of Myself*, written in his seventieth year, Kipling wrote: "My first impression is of daybreak, light and colour and golden and purple fruits at the level of my shoulder. This would be the memory of early morning walks to the Bombay fruit market with my *ayah* and later with my sister in her perambulator, and of our returns with our purchases piled high on the bows of it."

Like every English colonial official, Kipling's father could count on a reasonably good salary and the boy was provided with a Portuguese Catholic nurse who in the course of their walks would stop to offer up a prayer at a wayside shrine while he stood guard over his sister in her pram. Their Hindu bearer, Meeta, by contrast, would often take the two children into Hindu temples to worship his own gods. Daily familiarity with these two forms of religious observance helped to encourage the boy's open-minded attitude to spiritual matters. He had no preconceived views on religion nor any deep feeling for one particular faith in preference to another. Consequently he never established a firm belief in one God. His spiritual feelings were to remain vague and imprecise, hovering between a social conception of life based on a somewhat rickety framework of Christianity and an instinctive attraction, at a poetic level, for the mysticism of the East – in itself a curious jumble of Buddhism and Hinduism. Only by understanding these basic background facts can one really appreciate his early Indian stories and his later novel, *Kim*.

In the pages of the *Jungle Books* and *Kim* there are vivid evocations of the author's childhood impressions of busy streets, the stalls of the bazaars, the comings and goings of many races, the babble of languages and dialects expressing the most commonplace of casual exchanges or enshrining the profoundest of proverbs. It was all a dizzy, delightful dream, suddenly shattered when he was sent back to England to continue his education. Without warning the six-year-old boy and his sister were thrust into a new and bitter world.

Kipling wrote searchingly of his traumatic break with the past: "Then those days of strong light and darkness passed, and there was a time in a ship with an immense semi-circle blocking all vision on each side of her. (She must have been the old paddlewheel P. & O. *Ripon.*) There was a train across the desert (the Suez Canal was not yet opened) and a halt in it, and a small girl wrapped in a shawl on a seat opposite me, whose face stands out still. There was next a dark land, and a darker room full of cold, in one wall of which a white woman made naked fire, and I cried aloud with dread, for I had never before seen a grate."

According to modern theory such a trauma might well have led a small boy straight to the psychoanalyst's couch. The scars of this experience certainly remained within him but fortunately they were slight. From it emerged a man whose character was somewhat hard and unyielding, especially manifest in rigid political opinions that were clearly born of those years when lack of love and understanding engraved themselves deeply on his soul. Combined with this was a mistrust of women which, if it did not exhibit itself in the case of those few whom he genuinely loved, such as his wife and

mother, appears very clearly in his novels, where all the female characters possess something of the hardness and coldness of spirit that he detected immediately in that woman kneeling before the grate.

A childhood hell

Rudyard was to remain at Southsea for almost six years as boarder and foster-child to Captain and Mrs Holloway. The old man was virtually the slave of his wife, the terrifying Aunty Rosa. He would take Rudyard down to the shore to watch the ships at anchor and it was perhaps this early contact with the retired merchant navy captain that stimulated the boy's love for the sea, which inspired a number of his poems and one of his novels. These walks were a welcome relief from the tedium and torment of life at home, for already Rudyard was having to learn how best to steel himself and protect his younger sister from the harsh realities of a world in which there was little comfort or affection. Aunty Rosa, burning with pious zeal and a missionary's determination to educate this young savage from across the seas, refused to countenance the boy's open and frank manner of speaking his mind. As Kipling remembered it in later life: "It was an establishment run with the full vigour of the Evangelical as revealed to the Woman. I

had never heard of Hell, so I was introduced to it in all its terrors – I and whatever luckless little slavey might be in the house, whom severe rationing had led to steal food. Once I saw the Woman beat such a girl who picked up the kitchen poker and threatened retaliation. Myself I was regularly beaten. The Woman had an only son of twelve or thirteen as religious as she. I was a real joy to him, for when his mother had finished with me for the day (we slept in the same room) he took me on and roasted the other side."

Rudyard's attempt to escape from the greyness of everyday life through the books sent to him from India led to a gradual failing of eyesight which compelled him, even as a boy, to wear spectacles. Another form of respite came each December when Rudyard was invited to visit his aunt Georgina (Georgie), his mother's sister, married to the painter, Sir Edward Burne-Jones. After endless months of drudgery in the "House of Desolation" this winter holiday at The Grange, North End Road, was as he put it, "a paradise which I verily believe saved me. . . . At The Grange I had love and affection as much as the greediest, and I was not very greedy, could desire." It remained a treasured memory and when Kipling became a famous author he begged his aunt to send him the iron bell-pull from The Grange to attach to his own front door.

27

When Alice Kipling arrived to rescue her son from the house at Southsea his immediate reaction when she entered his bedroom was to raise his hand as if to ward off a blow. Aunty Rosa had a lot to answer for. In addition to his shortsightedness, for which she had been indirectly responsible, Rudyard suffered badly from insomnia, although he was to turn this to some advantage when he became a writer, working tirelessly into the small hours of the morning.

The carefree days with his mother following their reunion ended all too soon when he was enrolled at the United Services College at Westward Ho!, beautifully situated at Bideford Bay in north Devon. This public school had been founded in 1874 by a group of colonial army officers for their sons. Most of the pupils had, like Rudyard, been born in India. The headmaster, Cormell Price, was an old family friend but although Kipling knew him as "Uncle Crom", there was no favouritism and he was subjected to the same strict discipline as the other boys. These were to be impressionable, formative years. The school, though in no way comparable to the finest English public schools – it was, for one thing, much less expensive and could not afford special amenities or expect to attract the best teachers – instilled into its pupils an awareness of the traditional values of an educational system that was mainly concerned to turn out gentlemen suitable for a professional career in public service. The food was poor, the punishment harsh, the work demanding. Direct discipline was wielded by the teachers but summary justice could also be meted out by a handful of older boys who were entitled to certain recognised privileges. Such privileges, to which all new pupils naturally aspire, were assumed to be the rightful due of the senior boys, just as they would be for graduates of the school when they ventured out into the colonies and had dealings with those of lowlier birth and station.

The training which the United Services College gave its boys encouraged the team spirit rather than individuality and was based on the time-tested, typically British virtues of fortitude and self-sacrifice as preparation for the tough conditions that were likely, or rather certain, to be encountered in later life – especially when serving or travelling abroad.

Life at Westward Ho! was therefore rigorous but Kipling was by now better able to cope. At fourteen he was bigger than most of his companions and was therefore not singled out for bullying. He won respect for his swimming prowess and he made two close, lifelong friends in George Beresford and Lionel Dunsterville – the Triple Alliance of *Stalky & Co.*

Lahore apprenticeship

Towards the end of his second year at Westward Ho! the young Kipling suddenly conceived the idea of making a vocation out of writing. He began by buying a fat notebook with a black cloth cover and set to work composing a poem called *Inferno*, into which he put, "under appropriate torture, all my friends and most of the masters". The notion of taking a form of private revenge on some of his worst tormentors was ruined by his own indiscretion. Thinking himself alone, he would declaim his splendid verses aloud but the distinctive sound of his voice soon filtered down from hall and dormitory to the ears of the teachers.

Circumstances were now to dictate the course of his future career. His mother would have preferred him to go on to university but the doctors advised against it because of the bad state of his eyes. It was pretty obvious, moreover, to his elders and betters that the boy did not exactly display that measure of patient and diligent zeal demanded by Her Majesty's Civil Service and that he was better suited to a literary career. He himself was anxious to return to India and his parents were eventually persuaded that this was the best solution. Kipling described his arrival as follows: "So, at sixteen years and nine months, but looking four or five years older, and adorned with

28

real whiskers which the scandalised Mother abolished within one hour of beholding, I found myself at Bombay where I was born, moving among sights and smells whose meaning I knew not."

The bewilderment was temporary, for by accepting a journalistic career Kipling was immediately plunged back into the world that he dimly remembered from his childhood. All the memories of people and events that had been buried during his years of exile in England now came flooding back as he mingled with the colourful crowds in the streets and markets of Lahore where his family now lived. He soon proved himself an able newspaper reporter and became a respected member of local Anglo-Indian society. Initially he was welcomed as a member of the Punjab Club because of his family but soon he was known in his own right as the author of thought-provoking articles on local life and events. In 1885 he was admitted as a Freemason of the local Lodge, by special dispensation because he was under-age, eventually becoming its secretary.

At night, hounded by insomnia, Kipling would often slip out of the house and wander through the city streets in search of people and happenings that might provide source material for his writing. Such experiences remained firmly lodged in his mind and many of

them provided the framework of stories and novels which, by virtue of their frank realism, provoked lively and sometimes acrimonious discussion back in England. The books based on his Indian years challenged and upset many cherished beliefs of respectable men and women who were outraged at seeing their hallowed institutions exposed to the devastating glare of criticism and publicity. This brash young journalist wrote openly and unashamedly of what he saw and his descriptions of the seamier side of life in colonial India did not make for comfortable, genteel reading. Looking back on some of the grimmer aspects of army service, for example, he wrote later: "I came to realise the bare horrors of the private's life, and the unnecessary torments he endured on account of the Christian doctrine which lays down that 'the wages of sin is death'. It was counted impious that bazaar prostitutes should be inspected; or that the men should be taught elementary precautions in their dealings with them. This official virtue cost our Army in India nine thousand expensive white men a year always laid up from venereal disease. Visits to Lock Hospitals made me desire, as earnestly as I do today, that I might have six hundred priests – Bishops of the Establishment for a choice – to handle for six months precisely as the soldiers of my youth were handled."

Throughout his life Kipling's writing was characterised by this type of unflinching honesty. It was there in his first important prose work, *Plain Tales from the Hills*. In these stories Kipling vividly portrayed for his English readers a world of which they had little previous conception, a world in which pain, boredom, violence and suffering were real and commonplace.

A literary phenomenon

Indian experiences were invaluable to Kipling's development as a journalist and author, but he soon realised that in order to become a more than merely competent writer he would have to enlarge his human and cultural horizons by exploring new environments. To gather fresh experience, therefore, he readily accepted the *Pioneer's* offer to go around the world. In the spring of 1889 he sailed from Calcutta via Rangoon, Singapore, Hong-Kong and Yokohama for the United States and Britain. He treated it more as a holiday than a business assignment and did not get down to serious work until he arrived in New York. Although some of his articles and early works had already been published and reviewed in England he was not yet known in the United States. His hopes of making an immediate impact on the American

29

world of letters received a sharp setback in the course of an interview with the distinguished publisher Henry Harper who, after casting an indifferent eye over some of his articles, remarked icily: "Young man, this house is devoted to the production of literature." In London, however, he found much greater encouragement. Here he was considered as something of a literary phenomenon and stood on the brink of popular success.

One of the most endearing characteristics of Kipling was his close attachment to the family. Celebrity at the comparatively early age of 24 did not turn his head. He seemed almost unaware of the prestige he enjoyed among ordinary folk in the street, let alone in exclusive drawing-room society. He would deliberately shun publicity by seeking refuge within his own family circle. Although he never put his wife and children into his novels he spoke warmly and lovingly of them in *Something of Myself*. He married Caroline Balestier in 1892 and their life together was marked by a simple, strong bond of affection, cemented by their early struggles against economic hardship and later by their joint desire to invest all the money earned by his journalism and fiction as safely as possible. Kipling was to refer to the marriage partnership as a Committee of Ways and Means,

making it quite clear that in this area it was Caroline who took the real decisions.

The four years spent in Vermont were happy, though frequently punctuated by financial crises. The bank in which they had deposited all their money, about £2000, crashed soon after the wedding. The young couple, expecting their first child and left only with the clothes they had packed in their trunks, had to claim a refund from Cook's travel agency for the return tickets they had not used for their honeymoon. Compelled to remain in the States they rented an old house in Brattleboro for ten dollars a month from people . who had known Caroline's family when they had lived in the town. They called the house "Bliss Cottage". At the start there was some friction and misunderstanding between the Kiplings and their neighbours who, as patriotic Americans, could not comprehend why this eccentric Britisher had chosen to settle among them and how, by scribbling novels, he could reputedly "make as much as a hundred dollars out of a ten-cent bottle of ink". Gradually they thawed, however, and Kipling was afforded sufficient peace of mind and security to settle down in his tiny workroom at Bliss Cottage and turn out a stream of fine prose and poetry within four years. Among the works written in Vermont were the two *Jungle Books, The Seven Seas,*

the second set of *Barrack-Room Ballads* and Captains *Courageous.*

Apostle of conservatism

Kipling left America in the summer of 1896 and returned to England where he received a hero's welcome. He continued to write articles for leading daily papers and weekly magazines and was side-tracked into taking an active interest in politics. As a result of his conventional English education and Indian experiences it was natural for him to throw in his lot with the Conservatives who posed as the passionate defenders of tradition. His instinctively right-wing convictions were to be more deeply confirmed later in life when social and economic problems came to be hotly debated in parliament.

In these dying years of the 19th century Great Britain had attained the pinnacle of her power and prestige. The nation's domestic and foreign affairs were in the hands of the Tory party which had provided a succession of governments whose representatives were largely drawn from the landed gentry, accustomed to centuries of political power. Although the party contained its progressives the general view was that the Conservatives were singled out to govern by duty, right and tradition. In essence such sentiments were echoed by Kipling in his poems and in some of his lesser known prose works which were intended to instruct rather than to entertain.

In 1895 that symbol of British aristocracy, Robert Arthur Talbot Gascoyne-Cecil, 3rd Marquess of Salisbury, became Prime Minister for the third time. There was no stauncher opponent than Lord Salisbury to the growing agitation in support of the rights of the lower classes or to any movement for social reform. Radical opponents of the government argued for a tax on increasing land values, supporters of Home Rule waged their unrelenting battle for independence in Ireland, trade unionists campaigned for workers' representation in parliament and proclaimed the right of their members to strike for better conditions, socialists talked of nationalising property, and anarchists, more sweepingly, of abolishing it. All these diverse groups looked forward to some kind of radical change in society, but Kipling would have none of it. Decades later he was still painting a somewhat jaundiced picture of those people who wanted to build a new world. "In my wanderings," he wrote in *Something of Myself*, ". . . I had met several men and an occasional woman, whom I by no means loved. They were overly soft-spoken or blatant, and dealt in pernicious varieties

of safe sedition. For the most part they seemed to be purveyors of luxuries to the 'Aristocracy', whose destruction by painful means they loudly professed to desire. They derided my poor little Gods of the East, and asserted that the British in India spent violent lives 'oppressing' the Native. (This in a land where white girls of sixteen, at twelve or fourteen pounds per annum, hauled thirty and forty pounds weight of bath-water up four flights of stairs!) . . . Collaborating with these gentry was a mixed crowd of wide-minded, wide-mouthed Liberals, who darkened counsel with pious but disintegrating catch-words, and took care to live very well indeed. Somewhere, playing up to them, were various journals, not at all badly written, with a most enviable genius for perverting or mistaking anything that did not suit their bilious doctrine."

Such a comment, for all that it was partially justified, could only have come from a dedicated conservative and it was understandable that Kipling should have looked on a man such as Lord Salisbury as a paragon of perfection, personifying the writer's own heroic ideals of human endeavour. It was Salisbury's sincere and oft-proclaimed belief that a nation should be governed by men of wealth and high lineage, men who had the money and leisure to attain intellectual and cultural distinction and not be-

come involved in sordid and greedy struggles for power. Since only the aristocracy, in the literal sense of the term, possessed the necessary time and means to devote to such noble pursuits, it was essential that they should be entrusted with the governing of the nation. Kipling frequently endowed his fictional heroes with the virtues so admired by Salisbury and his colleagues. They might be high-ranking civil servants, colonels or just simple soldiers, but they all had one characteristic in common – a strong sense of patriotic duty. Furthermore, in his newspaper articles, he never concealed his admiration for the traditions that had made Britain strong, advocating conservative policies at home and abroad with fanatical ardour. An adoring public created a heroic image of him which his critics were powerless to tarnish. The caricatures of the writer, some of them extremely malicious, which circulated freely at the time in London, had little effect in dimming his popularity and reputation; indeed, they merely served to inflame public anger against those who sought to decry and abuse him.

The birth of Kim

Between 1899 and 1902 Kipling worked as a war correspondent in South Africa. In his determination to get as close as possible to the scene of battle he endured personal privation, recording events with a dispassionate honesty that surprised and angered many of his adherents at home. Although never questioning the rightness of the British cause in the Boer War, Kipling was deeply distressed and shocked by what he saw. His reports, far from glibly singing the praises of the British army, astonished his readers by frequently condemning gross blunders and atrocities; nor did he spare them grim details of service conditions. "Our own utter carelessness, officialdom and ignorance," he wrote, "were responsible for much of the death-rate. I have seen a Horse Battery 'dead to the wide' come in at midnight in raging rain and be assigned, by some idiot saving himself trouble, the site of an evacuated typhoid-hospital. Result — thirty cases after a month. I have seen men drinking raw Modder-river a few yards below where the mules were staling."

During his years in South Africa Kipling completed *Kim*, which was published in 1901. Generally regarded as his masterpiece, this novel is a form of homage to India and above all a tribute to the author's father who had spent most of his youth and adult life there. The character of the little Irish boy born in India who becomes an instrument of the great Imperial design was, if not directly inspired at least deepened in detail, by Kipling's Boer War experiences. Many young men who died for the Empire in South Africa were resurrected in the character of Kim.

It had been in the autumn of 1899 when on leave in London that Kipling had first revealed his plans for the new novel to the "Pater", who by that time was back in England for good. The draft of the book was in due course shown to his parents and it was his mother who suggested he should adopt the picaresque style of story-telling. "Don't you stand in your woolboots hiding behind Cervantes with *me*!" she exploded. "You *know* you couldn't make a plot to save your soul." So it was with the active assistance of his family that the character of Kim developed and the book took shape. In it he found the opportunity to recollect and relive all those happy childhood years in India, his parents giving him all the help they could by filling in background details of the times which for them too had been the happiest of their lives. Rudyard would write a few chapters, his mother would criticise them and his father would punctuate them with Indian words and phrases, varying the description of certain places, checking the correct form of proverbs, adding a detail of clothing or behaviour here and there, consistent with a particular character's racial origin. At one point, in a stable close to the village where they lived, John Kipling set up a kind of photographic studio where he prepared copper engravings of his own drawings, to be used as illustrations in the book.

The novel conveys a sense of that happy family co-operation. *Kim* was written largely for the author's own pleasure and it describes most colourfully and profoundly a colonial world that was already beginning to decline. The book appeared in the same year that Queen Victoria died. Twelve months later Lord Salisbury ceased to be Prime Minister. With the disappearance of these two key figures an age drew to a close. Henceforth, as the principles which had been his guidelines were gradually eroded, Kipling was to throw himself even more fiercely into the political arena, fighting for his conservative ideals, urged on by friends who often used him unashamedly for their own selfish purposes. It proved to be a sterile experience and very damaging to his reputation. Happily it was not for his political pronouncements that he would be remembered.

The Works of Kipling

"From the point of view of literature Mr Kipling is a genius who drops his aspirates. From the point of view of life, he is a reporter who knows vulgarity better than anyone has ever known it." OSCAR WILDE

In 1907 Rudyard Kipling won the Nobel Prize for Literature. The award was actually for "the most distinguished work of an idealistic tendency" and it was the first time it had ever gone to an English writer. "Idealism" was a strange word to use in reference to Kipling's work. Perhaps the judges admired his story-telling technique with its foursquare attitude to life as against the shallow, closeted romanticism, all sighs and tears, of many contemporary writers. "Realism" would have been more apt a term for a man who in addition to being a poet and writer of fiction was a polemical journalist and politician. Yet he never lost sight of certain personal ideals. Many of his works of fiction were intended to instruct as well as to entertain in that they glorified the British way of life. His adult heroes are personifications of the ideal Englishman, hard-working, full of initiative, dedicated to the acquisition of wealth as a due reward for proper conduct, utterly confident of eventual success. Kipling's fictional children, knowing that they are expected to follow in their fathers' footsteps, conform to the same standards of behaviour. Even the jungle animals, in their actions and words, prove themselves staunchly British!

Kipling's best works, from the literary point of view, are those he wrote in prose. These have tended to overshadow his enormous output of verse which has usually been somewhat curtly dismissed as tub-thumping, flag-waving nonsense. This is a wholly unfair judgment. It is true that some of the short, occasional poems, written to celebrate particular events, have not worn well with the passage of time. But comparatively few deal directly with the Imperial theme. Many, for example, are concerned with life at sea and sustain a high level of inspiration, with splendid rolling rhythms that convey a marvellous sense of the ocean's vastness and majesty.

It is impossible to divide Kipling's works into well defined categories. Intermingled with stories of pure fantasy are tales that are overtly didactic in purpose; and it is an equally profitless exercise to attempt grouping them together according to mood or background setting. In a brief survey such as this the most convenient way of analysing such a huge body of work is to look at it chronologically – a method which not only traces his artistic development but also shows how he derived inspiration from his travels, from major events and private incidents, from people he met and things he saw throughout a varied career.

Except for the short novels the titles of Kipling's books do not refer to a single tale but a collection of episodic stories which, taken together, may have a common mood or setting, forming component parts of a single picture. Often they feature the same characters and are accordingly, linked in theme and style.

Soldiers Three

This collection of short stories, featuring the adventures of three British soldiers stationed in India, was the first volume issued in the familiar grey covers by the Indian Railway Library in 1888 and was published in England in 1890. The sol-

33

Jacket for the first edition of Soldiers Three *(1888).*

diers are the Irishman Mulvaney, the Londoner Ortheris and the Yorkshireman Learoyd and the setting of the tales is usually the barracks which is their temporary home. These are no stylised soldiers but flesh-and-blood men – cynical, good-natured, undisciplined, rowdy, hard-drinking and rough-speaking. The seven stories do not make up a complete narrative but are more of a commentary on colonial army life as seen through the eyes of ordinary serving men. Military matters clearly fascinated Kipling but these tales were written primarily to make his readers aware of some of the realities of army life abroad, the love-hate attitude of the men towards their unit, their grudging respect for authority and the cameraderie that links them to one another and involves them with their superior officers. The language used by Kipling for the soldiers' dialogue is an absolutely faithful reproduction of actual barrack-room slang and local dialect, vividly suggesting the temperament and origins of the individual characters. Needless to say, it came as a shock to the reserved readers of the Victorian age who had been raised on much more delicate and tasteful literary fare.

Plain Tales from the Hills

Also brought out in serial form by the Indian Railway Library for sale on station bookstalls, *Plain Tales from the Hills* appeared in 1888. The stories, previously printed in *The Civil and Military Gazette* and the *Pioneer*, were now assured a much wider distribution. They were read by thousands of railway travellers, including English residents and middle-class Indians, and they also found their way abroad to England and the United States. The book contains forty stories, all roughly of uniform length (2,000–2,500 words), with an Indian or Anglo-Indian background. The central characters enact a single experience, described by Kipling with that incomparable verve and vivacity which created the myth of "magical India" for readers all round the world. Perhaps the most moving story is that of *Lispeth*, telling of a young Indian girl raised in an English mission who, after being deceived by an Englishman with whom she has fallen in love, returns to her own village, resuming the savage, primitive ways of her own people as if to blot out all memories of her "civilised" upbringing by the white ruling caste.

Included in this volume was Kipling's very first piece of imaginative writing, *The Gate of the Hundred Sorrows*, describing an opium den and its clients – a small masterpiece, all the more remarkable considering that the author was only nineteen.

Wee Willie Winkie and Under the Deodars

Wee Willie Winkie and Other Stories was also published in 1888. The title is derived from the central character of one of the tales, William Winkie, young son of the colonel commanding the 195th Regiment. The boy rides away from camp to rescue a white woman. They are captured by a band of enemy Afghans, but he manages to send a message back to the regiment and holds out bravely until help

comes. His reward for this act of courage is the agreement by the men of the regiment to drop the pet name "Winkie" and henceforth address him by his proper "man's" name of Pervival William Williams.

Another tale in this volume is *The Phantom Rickshaw*, a story of horror and pure fantasy, featuring a government official from Bombay named Pansay who, in the course of a sea trip from England to India, meets an officer's wife. They fall in love, and she gives up everything for her passion. But Pansay tires of her, and soon becomes engaged to a young girl. When the older woman dies of consumption Pansay, assuming responsibility for her death, begins seeing her in the streets sitting in a rickshaw, drawn by four brothers who had died of cholera. The hallucination, which he cannot shake off, drives him to madness. This story aptly reflects the sense of melancholy and isolation experienced by many Anglo-Indians, despite their material advantages.

Drums of the Fore and Aft, also in this volume, describes the adventures of a pair of drummer-boys,

Paperback edition (1888) of Under the Deodars.

scamps who make up for their smoking and scrapping in barracks, by marching alone, to the roll of their drums, against the enemy; so turning the tide of an apparently lost battle by British troops on the Afghan border.

Under the Deodars, a companion volume of short stories, though less successful as a whole, contains one powerful and humorous tale of marital deception and would-be adultery entitled *A Wayside Comedy*.

The Light that Failed

This book, almost a complete novel, was Kipling's first large-scale prose work, written in England after returning from India, and published in 1891. It appeared in two versions, a short form published in *Lippincott's Monthly Magazine* in January, with a happy ending, and a longer one, published by Macmillan, with an unambiguously tragic conclusion in March.

The central characters are Dick and Maisie. He is a painter of some repute who has produced illustrations of the British campaigns in the Sudan for various London papers. She is his childhood companion who, when he rediscovers her later in life, is haughty and indifferent. Dick's hopeless infatuation for Maisie leads him to a desperate search for artistic perfection, but his dreams are shattered when, as a result of a head wound received in the Egyptian campaign, he gradually goes blind. His finest painting, "Melancholia", done when he has lost his sight, is destroyed by his model Bessie, spitefully avenging herself on him for preventing her marrying one of his friends. When Maisie eventually returns to Dick and sees the formless blur of paint that he claims is his masterpiece, she abandons him for good. The painter eventually dies in an ambush in Africa.

Not all the characters in this book are successfully realised. Compared with Dick, Maisie is a lifeless, artificial figure. The descriptions of the Sudan fighting are uninspired, probably because Kipling had thus far never visited Egypt and was simply reconstructing battle scenes he had witnessed in India.

Most critics found the book brutal and coarse, advising the author to stick to the Indian stories that he did so well and not to waste time with experiments. But the public were enthusiastic about *The Light that Failed* and the book's popularity has not since waned. It has been transcribed for the stage and filmed three times, twice for the cinema and once for television.

The Finest Story in the World

The collection of stories that was published in 1893 under the title of *Many Inventions* contains what is arguably Kipling's most accomplished short story. The hero of *The Finest Story in the World* is Charles Mears, employed as a bank clerk in the City but cherishing literary ambitions. Charles meets a writer and offers to show him his first rather insipid, mediocre writings. At about this time, however, he undergoes an involuntary experience of metempsychosis, whereby his spirit passes into other bodies. He dreams of previous forms of existence, as a Viking and a

Phoenician slave, describing them verbally with so much richness of detail that his friend's interest is keenly aroused. Unfortunately, Charles proves quite incapable of committing his dream experiences to paper. Eventually love for a lower-class girl causes him to lose all contact with his dream personalities. Having tasted the passion that kills his memories, Charles never manages to write his masterpiece of the finest story in the world.

Alongside this tale is another tale set in the past – *The Lost Legion*. The action occurs during the Indian Mutiny and describes a British army unit compelled to spend an agonising night in the mountains of Afghanistan, awaiting an attack by a stronger enemy force. The soldiers, however, are inspired by ghosts of comrades killed in a previous engagement who put to flight the terrified Afghans, themselves filled with superstitious dread as a result of an ancient massacre in that very gorge.

The Jungle Book

Kipling's most famous book, written in Vermont, was published in 1894. The hero of three of the seven stories in the collection is Mowgli (which in local dialect means "the frog"), a small Indian boy brought up by the animals of the jungle. One night, Father Wolf of the Seeonee pack surprises the lame old tiger Shere Khan, who has been on the point of devouring a naked, brown "man-cub", abducted from a nearby village. The wolf saves the boy from the tiger and takes him to his lair to be raised with his own cubs. But in order to keep the man-cub he is obliged to seek the permission of the other animals. They give their consent only if two of their number, Baloo the brown bear and Bagheera the black panther, also agree. Baloo is the wise teacher of the Law of the Jungle and Bagheera is virtually the personification of the jungle itself, wild, cunning but softly spoken. Both animals are the inseparable companions of Mowgli during the fifteen years he lives in the jungle.

With the passing of time and the broadening of his knowledge Mowgli becomes lord of the jungle, mainly

Frontispiece for the first edition of The Jungle Book.

An illustration for The Jungle Book *(London, 1894).*

because his keen animal instincts are reinforced by human intelligence. As the boy grows he demonstrates his guile and bravery as he and his fellow animals encounter a variety of dangerous situations which initiate him into the realities of life. Two central episodes in this maturing process are his perilous adventures in the cold lairs of the Monkey-People and his fight to the death with Shere Khan the tiger. In the former case he is saved by the cunning of Baloo, Bagheera and Kaa the rock snake. In the latter adventure Mowgli manages to defeat the tiger by exercising his human intelligence. Shere Khan dies in a ravine, trampled under the feet of hundreds of buffaloes, frightened and stampeded by the boy and his wolf "brothers".

Rikki-Tikki-Tavi is the tale of the courageous little mongoose who fights the cobras Nag and Nagaina, intent upon killing the family living in the bungalow and garden which the reptiles regard as their rightful domain. The descriptions of the ferocious battles between Rikki-Tikki-Tavi and his deadly enemies are among the most vivid passages in all adventure fiction.

Kotick the White Seal is the story of a seal distinguished from all the other animals in the herd by his colour. Kotick becomes the leader of his people in searching for a new beach where they can find refuge from the annual bloodthirsty massacres of the Eskimo fishermen.

Another human character in *The Jungle Book* is Little Toomai, a boy who, like Mowgli, grows up among animals. The story of *Toomai and the Elephants*, filmed by the American director Robert Flaherty under the title of *Elephant Boy*, tells of the Indian child who is privileged to witness what no man has ever seen before – the dance of the elephants. Hiding among a group of old elephants owned by Petersen Sahib, Toomai slips away from camp on the night of a full moon and is joined by herds of elephants from every part of the jungle making their way to the Garo Hills where, at a trumpeted signal, they begin a fantastic dance that makes the earth tremble. When Toomai returns to camp the men pay tribute to the boy who has seen something denied to other men. The head driver of the elephants, Machua Appa, presents the lad to his colleagues, predicting that he will one day become the greatest elephant tracker in India.

The Jungle Book closes with a story called *Her Majesty's Servants*, which also has animals as the central characters – not the beasts of the jungle, however, but the domestic pack animals of a large military camp. Although this is not one of Kipling's most successful tales it gives him the opportunity to develop his ideas about law and government, for the rules regulating the animal kingdom are conceived as similar to those controlling the lives of the British people. Elephants, bullocks, horses, camels and mules follow the commands of their drivers, having no choice but to submit, in the last resort, to the will of the great Queen Victoria, empress of India. They too are Her Majesty's servants'

The Second Jungle Book

Published in 1895, this second collection tells of

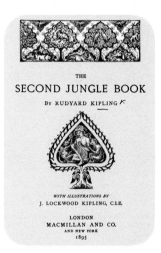

THE
SECOND JUNGLE BOOK
BY RUDYARD KIPLING

WITH ILLUSTRATIONS BY
J. LOCKWOOD KIPLING, C.I.E.

LONDON
MACMILLAN AND CO.
AND NEW YORK
1895

The Second Jungle Book
(London 1895).

Mowgli's later life and adventures, culminating in his return to human civilisation. The narrative is interspersed with other tales but the most beautiful and significant story is surely the last one in the book – *The Spring Running* – which describes with great sensitivity and skill the actual return of Mowgli to the world of men. The boy, now seventeen, is entranced, as he is every year, by the noise of the spring, a "vibrating boom" which pervades every part of the jungle, but senses that the

time has at last arrived for him to go back to his own people. Like all the jungle animals which, when spring comes, run for the sheer pleasure of movement, Mowgli now runs towards his own kind, towards love, towards his completeness as a human being – things the jungle can no longer ·give him. This has already been predicted by Akela, the old leader of the wolf pack, who, when fatally wounded after a furious fight against wild dogs, implores Mowgli to abandon those he has loved and served and to seek his future elsewhere. The moral is that although a man may be brought up in a jungle environment and learn its languages and laws he will essentially remain a man and must fulfil his destiny within human society.

The Second Jungle Book contains tales of other human characters besides Mowgli. The most moving of them, with an almost mystical feeling, is *The Miracle of Purum Bhagat*, about a native official who receives a knighthood but who renounces worldly wealth and celebrity to find truth in a contemplative life.

Purum Bhagat takes refuge in a deserted hillside shrine close to a village. Here he is honoured not only by the villagers but also by the animals of the jungle who are not afraid of him. It is they who warn him on a night of torrential rain that a landslip high up on the mountain threatens to engulf both his shrine and the little village below. Abandoning the life of meditation that he now realises has been induced by cold, inflexible self-love, the man runs, guided by deer and other mountain animals, to awaken the villagers, thus saving them from disaster. Purum Bhagat dies in the process but only after rediscovering, in human solidarity, the true meaning of life.

The little Eskimo Kotuko and his comrades are the central characters of *Quiquern*, an adventure set in the frozen wastes of the Arctic Circle. Kotuko has his first experience of hunting on the ice-cap, is lost in the middle of a tremendous blizzard, sees the Northern Lights and catches a glimpse of Quiquern, the phantom toothless dog. Finally he is guided home by mysterious spirits, together with a poor

Illustration from Captains Courageous *(1897).*

starving Eskimo girl he has met in his wanderings who becomes his life companion.

Captains Courageous

While living in America Kipling attended a memorial service to the fishermen of Gloucester, Massachusetts. Each year the town inhabitants gathered to pay tribute to those men who had died on the Newfoundland fishing grounds. Although it was a sad occasion the cere-

mony was virtually transformed into a festival honouring the bravery of the men of the fishing fleet, and the captains of the various ships proudly displayed the boxes of fish they had collected in their most recent voyage. It was against this background that Kipling conceived the idea of a novel that was to make him popular with children the world over – *Captains Courageous* (1891). Accompanied by Dr Conland, the family physician, who had sailed the Atlantic fishing grounds, Kipling visited all the inns of the town, chatting to old retired fishermen, noting down their experiences and gathering information about the methods of catching, preparing and conserving the cod that made up the bulk of their haul. In this way he stored away in his mind innumerable impressions and technical facts that he later wove into his narrative of ocean adventure.

Captains Courageous is the story of Harvey Cheyne, a spoilt boy from a wealthy family who ends up, by mischance, living with a shipload of fishermen and learning from them what life is really about. The tale begins on a large ocean liner where Harvey has been challenged to smoke an excessively strong cigar. When he starts to feel ill as a result of the combined effect of the cigar and the rolling motion of the ship, he goes up onto the deserted deck so as to avoid the gibes of the men who have been angered at his arrogance. It is a dark night and nobody sees Harvey lose his balance while leaning on the ship's rail and fall overboard. The boy recovers consciousness some hours later to find himself aboard the schooner of Captain Disko Troop, a rough sailor who entrusts him to the care of his son Dan, the cabinboy.

At this point Harveys' adventures yield place to a detailed account of ocean fishing and vivid descriptions of the vast expanse of sea in which the American trawler bobs like a nutshell. The sea and the ship are central to the theme of the book, which is a long story rather than a novel in the conventional sense and which has the range and rhythm of an epic poem. When he gets home Harvey finds his mother and father waiting for him. They cannot under-stand the profound change that has come over their son who left as an indolent boy and has now returned as a mature man, after an ex-perience that has completely altered his character. Face to face with his new son, the millionaire father who has built up his fortune by hard work decides to tell Harvey his own story in the hope that he will now have a son who can be a friend and an heir worthy of his trust.

Captains Courageous is un-fortunately crammed with didactic passages which weigh it down and impede the narrative flow. It is nevertheless redeemed by Kipling's inventiveness and creative genius and is mem-orable for those sections that describe shipboard life and the ever-changing moods of the sea.

Frontispiece of Stalky & Co. *(Toronto, 1899).*

Stalky & Co.

In 1896, back in England from the United States, Kip-ling settled in Rottingdean. The next year he wrote his ceremonial ode *Recessional* for the Diamond Jubilee of Queen Victoria. It heralded a new phase in his life, dur-ing which he produced a number of prose and poetic works in a moral, dogmatic vein. The novel *Stalky & Co.*, which was published in 1899, was deliberately intended "to educate the young".

The action takes place in a boys' public school, modelled on the United Services College at Westward Ho! where Kipling finished his formal education. The three principal characters are Stalky (in real life Lionel Dunsterville), M'Turk (George Beresford) and Beetle (Kipling himself). The book recounts their adventures – a succession of pranks, quarrels and hilarious occurrences that relieve the monotony of school life. This book too consists of a sequence of linked episodes rather than possessing a self-contained, unified plot. From them the reader obtains a vivid impression of the harsh, sometimes brutal discipline imposed in public schools of that period, even though Kipling himself described it as "the school before its time". The adventures of the three friends, often appearing more appropriate to a reformatory than a school, were criticised as being irreverent, distorted,

exaggerated and the like, and the two other members of the Triple Alliance were to produce their own versions of the truth as they remembered it. But Kipling was unrepentant. *Stalky & Co.* afforded him the opportunity of proclaiming one of his most fundamental beliefs – that the bullying by the more powerful and privileged members of the school, far from leaving scars of resentment in the minds of the victims, played a positive part in forming their character, teaching them stoicism and inspiring them with noble ideals. The same philosophy of the means justifying the ends is applied to the words and actions of the teachers. Kipling is sarcastic, sometimes grossly unfair in some of his descriptions of them but does not conceal the fact that they played an important role in his education. Thus in *Something of Myself* he was to write of the elderly Latin and Greek professor, named King in the novel, who ". . . taught me to loathe Horace for two years; to forget him for twenty, and then to love him for the rest of my days and through many sleepless nights".

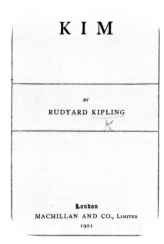

Frontispiece of first edition of Kim (1901).

Kim

Kim was the most successful of all Kipling's books, begun during the first few months of the Boer War in South Africa where he was serving as a war correspondent, and published in 1901 after a year of "incubation". The drafting of this book was for the author a rediscovery of the past; and he was aided in this quest by his father who was invaluable in reminding him of details that he had long forgotten. The great strength of *Kim* is not

Illustration by John Lockwood Kipling for Kim.

the story proper but the pulsating background of India, not just touched in or hinted at, as in so many of the short stories, but minutely described and re-evoked in a style which is a blend of reportage and social documentation, enriched by childhood memory and the shaping imagination of the mature writer.

Kim is an English boy who becomes a disciple of an old Tibetan lama who is journeying in search of the River of the Arrow which rises in a place where an arrow shot by the young god Buddha once fell. The lama wishes to travel there in order to free himself from the Wheel of Things and thus get rid of worldly passions. With this intention he has left his monastery and gone to India. In front of the Lahore museum he meets Kim, the "Little Friend of all the World", son of an Irish sergeant who has killed himself with alcohol and opium and a mother who disappeared while he was a baby. Kim has been brought up by an Indian woman who wishes him to go off on a mission, telling him that his fate is linked with that of a Red Bull on a green field — the insignia of his father's regiment. So the lama and the boy set off in quest of peace. Their travels provide the author with an excuse to describe India, its merchants, its holy men, the old soldiers of the British Empire, the corrupt priests of various religious sects, the dusty roads crowded with wagons, and, underlying everything, the system of espionage or Great Game into which Kim is unwittingly drawn. To be involved in this spy network he has to leave the lama and attend a school where he learns to read and write, thus receiving an English education which will enrich him without destroying his "Indian" soul.

The second part of the novel almost assumes the qualities of a thriller as Kim becomes involved in a series of dark intrigues perpetrated by the enemies of Britain who are fomenting disorder and rebellion in northern India. The novel ends when the lama finds his River, rescuing Kim from drowning, but by now the boy is no longer the same Little Friend of all the World but a small link in the ugly chain of espionage, a little cigar-puffing rascal who will grow up to be a true Anglo-Indian, one of those who will be expected to view India only as the most glittering jewel in the Imperial crown.

Kim is the literary projection of Kipling's own desires and intuitions. Despite the weakness of the spy theme the story of the boy and the lama is the most complete of his novels, and its success was an important step towards winning the Nobel Prize for Literature six years later.

43

Drawing by Rudyard Kipling for his Just So Stories.

Just So Stories

The delightful animal tales collected together under the title *Just so Stories* were published in 1902. They had, however, been written at intervals over the previous five years. Kipling had meant them to be recited aloud rather than read, choosing an artificial style suitable for children which echoed the cadences of the lullabies and tales of his Indian childhood. We have a first-hand account of how these animal stories originated and developed from Angela Mackail (later Angela Thirkell), the grand-daughter of Edward and Georgina Burne-Jones, who was a close friend of Kipling's elder daughter Josephine.

"During those long warm summers," she wrote, "Cousin Ruddy used to try out the *Just So Stories* on a nursery audience. Sometimes Josephine and I would be invited into his study, a pleasant bow-windowed room, where Cousin Ruddy sat at his work-table looking exactly like the portrait of him that Uncle Phil painted.

"The *Just So Stories* are a poor thing in print compared with the fun of hearing them

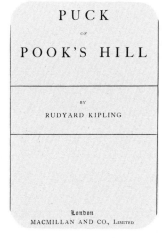

First edition of Puck of Pook's Hill *(London, 1906).*

told in Cousin Ruddy's deep unhesitating voice. There was a ritual about them, each phrase having its special intonation which had to be exactly the same each time and without which the stories are dried husks. There was an inimitable cadence, and emphasis of certain words, an exaggeration of certain phrases, a kind of intoning here and there which made his telling unforgettable."

This narrative technique, expressly designed for small children, has stood the test of time. The first edition of the book was illustrated by the author himself and he also wrote the extended picture captions. They are very simple drawings, in keeping with the themes, explaining exactly what is happening. The eleven stories are drawn from the realm of Indian fable. In the first, *How the Whale Got his Throat*, the huge whale travels the ocean, gulping down fish to satisfy his hunger, until he meets a 'stute fish who suggests the whale should try tasting Man. So the whale swallows a shipwrecked mariner who spends hour after hour dancing in the animal's stomach. Eventually, exhausted by the tickling sensation, the whale disgorges him on the seashore near his home. But the raft remains stuck in its throat. "From that day on," explains Kipling, "the grating in his throat, which he could neither cough up nor swallow down, prevented him from eating anything except very, very small fish; and that is the reason why whales nowadays never eat men or boys or little girls."

The most charming story of all is *The Elephant's Child* which tells how the elephant got its trunk. Originally he had only a "blackish, bulgy nose, as big as a boot", but because he was so inquisitive he was spanked by his father, his mother, his tall aunt the ostrich, his tall uncle the giraffe, his broad aunt the hippopotamus and his hairy uncle the baboon. All he wants to know is what the crocodile has for dinner and he soon discovers this on the banks of the "great, grey-green greasy Limpopo river". The crocodile tries to pull the baby elephant into the river but he stands firm, his nose getting longer and longer until the crocodile lets go. He wraps it in banana leaves and trails it in the water to cool but it does not shrink; and he returns home with a five-foot trunk.

Other tales in the *Just So Stories* offer equally ingenious explanations as to *How the Rhinoceros Got his Skin* and *How the Leopard Got his Spots*.

Puck of Pook's Hill

In 1906 Kipling published the complete collection of instructive stories that he had written over the years

Frontispiece for Puck of Pook's Hill *(1906)*.

and which he now entitled *Puck of Pook's Hill*. These tales were his way of telling children something about British history and the origins of the traditions that made the nation great. Dan and Una, brother and sister, are performing bits of Shakespeare's comedy *Midsummer Night's Dream* to an audience of three cows in a meadow. As the young actors play the scene of the enchantment of Bottom – Dan playing Puck, Bottom and the fairies, Una Titania – the bushes part and out of them steps a "small, brown, broad-shouldered, pointy-eared person with a snub nose, slanting blue eyes, and a grin that ran right across his freckled face." It is Puck himself and he undertakes to introduce the children to some of the characters of early English history. Puck's magic enables them to see many of the exciting events that have occurred over the past two thousand years – things they will forget as soon as the fairy vanishes and they return home. A vivid gallery of personages and a succession of epic events save the book from becoming too serious and stuffy in tone, and although

there is a good deal more fantasy than fact it represents a pleasant and painless way of teaching history.

In the first story of *Weland's Sword*, Kipling recounts the adventures of the ancient pagan god Weland, who remains hidden in the English woods even when all the idols have been destroyed with the advent of Christianity. Instead of making his escape through the trees, as many of his companions have done, Weland continues living under the disguise of a smith. He cannot return to Valhalla because he is under a magic spell. Only when a human recognises his true identity will he be permitted to rejoin his comrades among the servants of the great god Thor. The spell is broken by the monastic novice Hugh who receives as his reward a "dark-grey, wavy-lined sword" made by Weland, cooled in running water and evening dew, its blade carved with prophetic runes.

The sword also makes an appearance in two other stories, *Young Men at the Manor* and *Old Men at Pevensey*, which are set in the reign of William the

Conqueror. But the most remarkable story is *A Centurion of the Thirtieth*, about a Roman centurion named Parnesius, born in England and detailed to help defend Hadrian's Wall against invaders from the north. On the other side are Rome's enemies, the Picts, but Parnesius sees them as brothers, from the same island stock. This is an original way of presenting the Roman occupation, as a single soldier's crisis of conscience. Parnesius is a hero with human problems arising from a confrontation between an occupying power and a native culture, suggesting a parallel with the British in India.

The liberties Kipling took with historical fact are justified by the creative power of his imagination and *Puck of Pook's Hill* emerges as an intriguing blend of reality and myth.

Rewards and Fairies

Kipling tried to repeat the success of *Puck of Pook's Hill* four years later with *Rewards and Fairies*, a series of eleven stories in similar vein. This time, however, the mixture of history and legend is far less convincing, partly because the tales are too adult, partly because they show too many obvious signs of slackness and loose concentration. It was at about this time, too, that Kipling began to indulge in a militant political career, drawing him away from literature. The book does, however, contain some fine verses, including the famous poem entitled *If* –

Something of Myself and minor prose works

Something of Myself was a diary written by Kipling during his last years and published posthumously in 1937. It is distinguished by its sparkling style and warm, human tone. The pages in which he evokes his South African experiences in the Boer War constitute a particularly striking example of brilliant, objective journalism.

In later life, after receiving his Nobel Prize, Kipling turned out a host of minor prose works, the majority of which were essays, journalistic reports or political pamphlets. The despatches he sent from the front during the First World War, especially those collected and published in 1917 under the title of *The War in the Mountains*, based on experiences in Italy, are outstanding. In later years he had clearly lost much of his flair and originality, political work not proving a spur to fresh artistic endeavour.

By and large Kipling was most successful as a storyteller. The two *Jungle Books* are essentially collections of short stories and even *Kim*, his most celebrated novel, lacks a continuous narrative thread, the various episodes not following one another in any logical sequence. The difference between his short stories and his novels was, in Marcel Brion's opinion, basically a change of rhythm, the pace of the former being rapid, breathless and exciting, the latter slower, more measured, often attaining the grandeur of epic poetry. Most unbiased readers will agree that it is in the short stories that Kipling is at his best.

Poetical works

Kipling wrote a great many poems, for the most part short pieces originally published in daily papers and for that reason difficult to classify. The best known collections, however, are the *Barrack-Room Ballads* and *The Seven Seas*.

Published in book form in 1892, the *Barrack-Room Ballads* represent Kipling's tribute to the ordinary British soldier – Tommy Atkins. The dedication reads:

"I have made for you a song, And it may be right or wrong, But only you can tell me if it's true; I have tried for to explain Both your pleasure and your pain, And, Thomas, here's my best respects to you."

Depicting the soldier's life in many varied aspects – work, play and death – some of these poems, such as *Tommy*, *Gunga Din* and *Mandalay*, are probably better known to the average reader than the sonnets of Shakespeare or the lyric verses of the romantic poets. Most of the verses in the second series also appeared in *The Seven Seas*, published in 1896. The linking thread of these poems is the ocean lapping the shores of the lands belonging to the British Empire, and essenti-

THE SEVEN SEAS

BY RUDYARD KIPLING

METHUEN AND CO.
36 ESSEX STREET, W.C.
LONDON
1896

First edition of The Seven Seas
(London, 1896).

ally they celebrate the exploits of those who have crossed the seas in the service of the mother country. In the sequence of poems entitled *A Song of the English* the voices of the dead are heard:

"We have fed our sea for a thousand years And she calls us, still unfed, Though there's never a wave of all her waves But marks our English dead."

The authentic voice of Kipling rings out in the last poem, *England's Answer*:

"Go to your work and be strong, halting not in your ways, Baulking the end half-won for an instant dole of praise. Stand to your work and be wise – certain of sword and pen, Who are neither children nor Gods, but men in a world of men!"

In the *Envoi* to *The Seven Seas*, Kipling strikes a quieter, more pensive note in a personal vision of a paradise where work is still exalted:

"When Earth's last picture is painted and the tubes are twisted and dried,
When the oldest colours have faded, and the youngest critic has died.
We shall rest, and, faith, we shall need it – lie down for an aeon or two,
Till the Master of All Good Workmen shall put us to work anew.

"And those that were good shall be happy: they shall sit in a golden chair;
They shall splash at a ten-league canvas with brushes of comets' hair.
They shall find real saints to draw from – Magdalene, Peter, and Paul;
They shall work for an age at a sitting and never be tired at all!"

The Art of the Punjab

Kipling was familiar with the art of the Punjab because his father was curator of the famous art museum at Lahore.

Above: *the Maharajah Kharak Singh hunting with his retainers – a famous 19th-century miniature of the Kangra school. This was one of the main centres of Indian painting in the Punjab, the Himalayan state where Kipling lived from 1882 until 1889.*

49

Facing page: *the Maharajah Gulab Singh (Kangra miniature of 1806). The Kangra school, developed in the Punjab around 1740, was the last major manifestation of traditional Rajput painting which had flourished in mediaeval India under the patronage of local rulers.*

The perfect expression of the aristocratic society producing it, Rajput painting blended naturalism with an idealistic vision of life, the world and mankind, represented according to canons of spiritual beauty. Many of the paintings extolled the pleasures of love. **Above**, **left**: Lady with her Sikh Lover *(miniature 1830)*. **Above**, **right**: Girl Awaiting her Lover *(Kangra gouache, end of 19th-century)*.

Above: Spring Festival *(Kangra gouache of 1800). Characterised by fluid rhythms and splendid coloration, the Kangra style is rich in emotive force and lyricism, the artists attempting to translate poetry into art.* **Right**: *a princess smokes a narghile while musicians wait to play (miniature of 1820).*

53

Below: Valmiki Reads the Ramayana to the People of the Himalayas *(Kangra gouache of 1805). The ancient Sanskrit poem, the* Ramayana, *celebrates the deeds of Rama, one of the incarnations of the god Vishnu. The work is traditionally attributed to Valmiki, whom Indians regard as their foremost "poet of art".*

The painters of the Kangra school often found inspiration for their works in the legends related to the cult of Radha-Krishna, dating from the 15th century. Krishna was the eighth incarnation of Vishnu, and Radha, his devoted wife, represents the human spirit which always strives to raise itself to the highest level of beatitude. **Right**: Radha and Krishna in a Garden *(gouache of 1840).*

On this page are illustrated typical articles of silver jewellery created by Punjabi craftsmen in the 19th century. **Left, above**: *a bracelet from Lahore.* **Left, below**: *a necklace composed of coin amulets.* **Right, top to bottom**: *a gold ring with pearls, and two bracelets. Indian goldsmith's ware of the 19th century did not have a unified style; alongside huge jewels are smaller objects of delicate workmanship, fashioned either by the filigree or granulation method.*

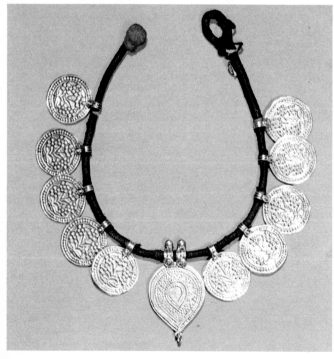

A Kipling Anthology

Lispeth: from Plain Tales from the Hills

The beautiful Indian girl Lispeth encounters white civilisation and falls in love. Misunderstood, betrayed and hurt, she returns to her own people.

She was the daughter of Sonoo, a Hill-man of the Himalayas, and Jadeh his wife. One year their maize failed, and two bears spent the night in their only opium poppy-field just above the Sutlej Valley on the Kotgarh side; so, next season, they turned Christian, and brought their baby to the Mission to be baptised. The Kotgarh Chaplain christened her Elizabeth and "Lispeth" is the Hill or *pahari* pronunciation.

Later, cholera came into the Kotgarh Valley and carried off Sonoo and Jadeh, and Lispeth became half servant, half companion, to the wife of the then Chaplain of Kotgarh. This was after the reign of the Moravian missionaries in that place, but before Kotgarh had quite forgotten her title of "Mistress of the Northern Hills".

Whether Christianity improved Lispeth, or whether the gods of her own people would have done as much for her under any circumstances, I do not know; but she grew very lovely. When a Hill-girl grows lovely, she is worth travelling fifty miles over bad ground to look upon. Lispeth had a Greek face – one of those faces people paint so often, and see so seldom. She was of a pale, ivory colour, and, for her race, extremely tall. Also, she possessed eyes that were wonderful; and had she not been dressed in the abominable print-cloths affected by Missions, you would, meeting her on the hillside unexpectedly, have thought her the original Diana of the Romans going out to slay.

Lispeth took to Christianity readily, and did not abandon it when she reached womanhood, as do some Hill-girls. Her own people hated her be-

cause she had, they said, become a white woman and washed herself daily; and the Chaplain's wife did not know what to do with her. One cannot ask a stately goddess, five feet ten in her shoes, to clean plates and dishes. She played with the Chaplain's children and took classes in the Sunday School, and read all the books in the house, and grew more and more beautiful, like the Princesses in fairy tales. The Chaplain's wife said that the girl ought to take service in Simla as a nurse or something "genteel". But Lispeth did not want to take service. She was very happy where she was.

When travellers – there were not many in those years – came in to Kotgarh, Lispeth used to lock herself into her own room for fear they might take her away to Simla, or out into the unknown world.

One day, a few months after she was seventeen years old, Lispeth went out for a walk. She did not walk in the manner of English ladies – a mile and a half out, with a carriage-ride back again. She covered between twenty and thirty miles in her little constitutionals, all around and about, between Kotgarh and Narkanda. This time she came back at full dusk, stepping down the breakneck descent into Kotgarh with something heavy in her arms. The Chaplain's wife was dozing in the drawing-room when Lispeth came in breathing heavily and very exhausted with her burden. Lispeth put it down on the sofa, and said simply, "This is my husband. I found him on the Bagi Road. He has hurt himself. We will nurse him, and when he is well your husband shall marry him to me."

This was the first mention Lispeth had ever made of her matrimonial views, and the Chaplain's wife shrieked with horror. However, the man on the sofa needed attention first. He was a young Englishman, and his head had been cut to the bone by something jagged. Lispeth said she had found him down the hillside, and had brought him in. He was breathing queerly and was unconscious.

He was put to bed and tended by the Chaplain, who knew something of medicine; and Lispeth waited outside the door in case she could be useful. She explained to the Chaplain that this was the man she meant to marry; and the Chaplain and his wife lectured her severely on the impropriety of her conduct. Lispeth listened quietly, and repeated her first proposition. It takes a great deal of Christianity to wipe out uncivilised Eastern instincts, such as falling in love at first sight. Lispeth, having found the man she worshipped, did not see why she should keep silent as to her choice. She was going to nurse that Englishman until he was well enough to marry her. This was her programme.

After a fortnight of slight fever and inflammation, the Englishman recovered coherence and thanked the Chaplain and his wife, and Lispeth – especially Lispeth – for their kindness. He was a traveller in the East, he said – they never talked about "globe-trotters" in those days, when the P. & O. fleet was young and small – and had come from Dehra Dun to hunt for plants and butterflies among the Simla hills. No one at Simla, therefore, knew anything about him. He fancied that he must have fallen over the cliff while reaching out for a fern on a rotten tree-trunk, and that his coolies must have stolen his baggage and fled. He thought he would go back to Simla when he was a little stronger. He desired no more mountaineering.

He made small haste to go away, and recovered his strength slowly. Lispeth objected to being advised either by the Chaplain or his wife; therefore the latter spoke to the Englishman, and told him how matters stood in Lispeth's heart. He laughed a good deal, and said it was very pretty and romantic, but, as he was engaged to a girl at Home, he fancied that nothing would happen. Certainly he would behave with discretion. He did that. Still he found it very pleasant to talk to Lispeth, and walk with Lispeth, and say nice things to her, and call her pet names while he was getting strong enough to go away. It meant nothing at all to him, and everything in the world to Lispeth. She was very happy while the fortnight lasted, because she had found a man to love.

Being a savage by birth, she took no trouble to hide her feelings, and the Englishman was amused. When he went away, Lispeth walked with him up the Hill as far as Narkanda, very troubled and very miserable. The Chaplain's wife, being a good Christian and disliking anything in the shape of fuss or scandal – Lispeth was beyond her management entirely – had told the Englishman to tell Lispeth that he was coming back to marry her. "She is but a child, you know, and, I fear, at heart a heathen," said the Chaplain's wife. So all the twelve miles up the Hill the Englishman, with his arm round Lispeth's waist, was assuring the girl that he would come back and marry her; and Lispeth made him promise over and over again. She wept on the Narkanda Ridge till he had passed out of sight along the Muttiani path.

Then she dried her tears and went in to Kotgarh again, and said to the Chaplain's wife, "He will come back and marry me. He has gone to his own people to tell them so." And the Chaplain's wife soothed Lisbeth and said, "He will come back." At the end of two months Lispeth grew impatient, and was told that the Englishman had gone over the seas to England. She knew where England was, because she had read little geography primers; but, of course, she had no conception of the nature of the sea, being a Hill-girl. There was an old puzzle-map of the World in the house. Lispeth had played with it when she was a child. She unearthed it again, and put it together of evenings, and cried to herself, and tried to imagine where her Englishman was. As she had no ideas of distance or steamboats her notions were somewhat wild. It would not have made the least difference had she been perfectly correct; for the Englishman had no intention of coming back to marry a Hill-girl. He forgot all about her by the time he was butterfly-hunting in Assam. He wrote a book on the East afterwards. Lispeth's name did not appear there.

At the end of three months Lispeth made daily pilgrimage to Narkanda to see if her Englishman was coming along the road. It gave her comfort, and the Chaplain's wife finding her happier thought that she was getting over her "barbarous and most indelicate folly". A little later the walks ceased to help Lispeth, and her temper grew very bad. The Chaplain's wife thought this a profitable time to let her know the real state of affairs – that the Englishman had only promised his love to keep her quiet – that he had never meant anything, and that it was wrong and improper of Lispeth to think of marriage with an Englishman, who was of a superior clay, besides being promised in marriage to a girl of his own people. Lispeth said that all this was clearly impossible because he had said he loved her, and the Chaplain's wife had, with her own lips, asserted that the Englishman was coming back.

"How can what he and you said be untrue?" asked Lispeth.

"We said it as an excuse to keep you quiet, child," said the Chaplain's wife.

"Then you have lied to me," said Lispeth, "you and he?"

The Chaplain's wife bowed her head, and said nothing. Lispeth was silent too for a little time; then she went out down the valley, and returned in the dress of a Hill-girl – infamously dirty, but without the nose-stud and ear-rings. She had her hair braided into the long pigtail, helped out with black thread, that Hill-women wear.

"I am going back to my own people," said she. "You have killed Lispeth. There is only left old Jadeh's daughter – the daughter of a *pahari* and the servant of *Tarka Devi*. You are all liars, you English."

By the time that the Chaplain's wife had recovered from the shock of the announcement that Lispeth had 'verted to her mother's gods the girl had gone; and she never came back.

She took to her own unclean people savagely, as if to make up the arrears of the life she had stepped out of; and, in a little time, she married a wood-cutter who beat her after the manner of *paharis*, and her beauty faded soon.

"There is no law whereby you can account for the vagaries of the heathen," said the Chaplain's wife, "and I believe that Lispeth was always at heart an infidel." Seeing she had been taken into the Church of England at the mature age of five weeks, this statement does not do credit to the Chaplain's wife.

Lispeth was a very old woman when she died. She had always a perfect command of English, and when she was sufficiently drunk could sometimes be induced to tell the story of her first love-affair.

It was hard then to realise that the bleared, wrinkled creature, exactly like a wisp of charred rag, could ever have been "Lispeth of the Kotgarh Mission".

Excerpt from The Light that Failed

A furtive and unsuccessful childhood kiss opens new worlds to Dick and Maisie.

FROM CHAPTER I

Maisie turned, the revolver in her hand, just in time to see Amomma scampering away from the pebbles Dick threw after him. Nothing is sacred to a billy-goat. Being well fed and the adored of his mistress, Amomma had naturally swallowed two loaded pin-fire cartridges. Maisie hurried up to assure herself that Dick had not miscounted the tale.

"Yes, he's eaten two."

"Horrid little beast! Then they'll joggle about inside him and blow up, and serve him right. . . . Oh, Dick! have I killed you?"

Revolvers are tricky things for young hands to deal with. Maisie could not explain how it had happened, but a veil of reeking smoke separated her from Dick, and she was quite certain that the pistol had gone off in his face. Then she heard him sputter, and dropped on her knees beside him, crying, "Dick, you aren't hurt, are you? I didn't mean it."

"Of course you didn't," said Dick, coming out of the smoke and wiping his cheek. "But you nearly blinded me. That powder stuff stings awfully." A neat little splash of grey lead on a stone showed where the bullet had gone. Maisie began to whimper.

"Don't," said Dick, jumping to his feet and shaking himself. "I'm not a bit hurt."

"No, but I might have killed you," protested Maisie, the corners of her mouth drooping. "What should I have done then?"

"Gone home and told Mrs Jennett." Dick grinned at the thought; then, softening, "Please don't worry about it. We've got to get back to tea. I'll take the revolver for a bit."

Maisie would have wept on the least encouragement, but Dick's indifference, albeit his hand was shaking as he picked up the pistol, restrained her. She lay panting on the beach while Dick methodically bombarded the breakwater. "Got it at last!" he exclaimed, as a lock of weed flew from the wood.

"Let me try," said Maisie imperiously. "I'm all right now."

They fired in turns till the rickety little revolver nearly shook itself to pieces, and Amomma the outcast – because he might blow up at any moment – browsed in the background and wondered why stones were thrown at him. Then they found a balk of timber floating in a pool which was commanded by the seaward slope of Fort Keeling, and they sat down together before this new target.

"Next holidays," said Dick, as the now thoroughly fouled revolver kicked wildly in his hand, "we'll get another pistol – central fire – that will carry farther."

"There won't be any next holidays for me," said Maisie. "I'm going away."

"Where to?"

"I don't know. My lawyers have written to Mrs Jennett, and I've got to be educated somewhere – in France, perhaps – I don't know where; but I shall be glad to go away."

"I shan't like it a bit. I suppose I shall be left. Look here, Maisie, is it really true you're going? Then these holidays will be the last I shall see anything of you; and I go back to school next week. I wish – "

The young blood turned his cheeks scarlet. Maisie was picking grass-tufts and throwing them down the slope at a yellow sea-poppy nodding all

Lispeth, *a terracotta relief by John Lockwood Kipling.*

by itself to the illimitable levels of the mudflats and the milk-white sea beyond.

"I wish," she said, after a pause, "that I could see you again some time. You wish that too?"

"Yes, but it would have been better if – if – you had – shot straight over there – down by the breakwater."

Maisie looked with large eyes for a moment. And this was the boy who only ten days before had decorated Amomma's horns with cut-paper ham-frills and turned him out, a bearded derision, among the public ways! Then she dropped her eyes: this was not the boy.

"Don't be stupid," she said reprovingly, and with swift instinct attacked the side-issue. "How selfish you are! Just think what I should have felt if that horrid thing had killed you! I'm quite miserable enough already."

"Why? Because you're going away from Mrs Jennett?"

"No."

"From me, then?"

No answer for a long time. Dick dared not look at her. He felt, though he did not know, all that the past four years had been to him, and this the more acutely since he had no knowledge to put his feelings in words.

"I don't know," she said. "I suppose it is."

"Maisie, you must know. *I'm* not supposing."

"Let's go home," said Maisie weakly.

But Dick was not minded to retreat.

"I can't say things," he pleaded, "and I'm awfully sorry for teasing you about Amomma the other day. It's all different now, Maisie, can't you see? And you might have told me that you were going, instead of leaving me to find out."

"You didn't. I did tell. Oh, Dick, what's the use of worrying?"

"There isn't any; but we've been together years and years, and I didn't know how much I cared."

"I don't believe you ever did care."

"No, I didn't; but I do – I care awfully now. Maisie," he gulped – "Maisie, darling, say you care too, please."

"I do; indeed I do; but it won't be any use."

"Why?"

"Because I am going away."

"Yes, but if you promise before you go. Only say – will you?" A second "darling" came to his lips more easily than the first. There were few endearments in Dick's home or school life; he had to find them by instinct. Dick caught the little hand blackened with the escaped gas of the revolver.

"I promise," she said solemnly; "but if I care, there is no need for promising?"

"And you do care?" For the first time in the past few minutes their eyes met and spoke for them who had no skill in speech. . . .

"Oh, Dick, don't! please don't! It was all right when we said good-morning; but now it's all different!" Amomma looked on from afar. He had seen his property quarrel frequently, but he had never seen kisses exchanged before. The yellow sea-poppy was wiser, and nodded its head approvingly. Considered as a kiss, that was a failure, but since it was the first, other than those demanded by duty, in all the world that either had ever given or taken, it opened to them new worlds, and every one of them glorious, so that they were lifted above the consideration of any worlds at all, especially those in which tea is necessary, and sat still, holding each other's hands and not saying a word.

"You can't forget now," said Dick at last. There was that on his cheek that stung more than gunpowder.

"I shouldn't have forgotten anyhow," said Maisie, and they looked at each other and saw that each was changed from the companion of an hour ago to a wonder and mystery they could not understand.

Excerpts from Captains Courageous

Young Harvey Cheyne, heir to a large fortune, falls into the sea and is picked up by a fishing vessel. The hard life at sea makes a real man of him.

FROM CHAPTER I

"You like my cigar, eh?" the German asked, for Harvey's eyes were full of tears.

"Fine, full flavour," he answered through shut teeth. "Guess we've slowed down a little, haven't we? I'll skip out and see what the log says."

"I might if I vas you," said the German.

Harvey staggered over the wet decks to the nearest rail. He was very unhappy; but he saw the deck-steward lashing chairs together, and since he had boasted before the man that he was never seasick, his pride made him go aft to the second-saloon deck at the stern, which was finished in a turtle-back. The deck was deserted, and he crawled to the extreme end of it near the flag-pole. There he doubled up in limp agony, for the Wheeling "stogie" joined with the surge and jar of the screw to sieve out his soul. His head swelled; sparks of fire danced before his eyes; his body seemed to lose weight, while his heels wavered in the breeze. He was fainting from seasickness, and a roll of the ship tilted him over the rail on to the smooth lip of the turtle-back. Then a low, grey mother-wave swung out of the fog, tucked Harvey under one arm, so to speak, and pulled him off and away to leeward; the great green closed over him, and he went quietly to sleep.

He was roused by the sound of a dinner-horn such as they used to blow at a summer-school he had once attended in the Adirondacks. Slowly he remembered that he was Harvey Cheyne, drowned and dead in mid-ocean, but was too weak to fit things together. A new smell filled his nostrils; wet and clammy chills rand down his back, and he was helplessly full of salt water. When he opened his eyes, he perceived that he was still on the top of the sea, for it was running round him in silver-coloured hills, and he was lying on a pile of half-dead fish, looking at a broad human back clothed in a blue jersey.

"It's no good," thought the boy. "I'm dead, sure enough, and this thing is in charge."

He groaned, and the figure turned its head, showing a pair of little gold rings half hidden in curly black hair.

"Aha! You feel some pretty well now?" it said. "Lie still so. We trim better."

With a swift jerk he sculled the flickering boat-head on to a foamless sea that lifted her twenty full feet only to slide her into a glassy pit beyond. But this mountain-climbing did not interrupt blue-jersey's talk. "Fine good job, *I* say, that I catch you. Eh, wha-at? Better good job, *I* say, your boat not catch me. How you come to fall out?"

"I was sick," said Harvey; "sick, and couldn't help it."

"Just in time I blow my horn, and your boat she yaw a little. Then I see you come all down. Eh, wha-at? I think you are cut into baits by the screw, but you dreeft – dreeft to me, and I make a big feesh of you. So you shall not die this time."

"Where am I?" said Harvey, who could not see that life was particularly safe where he lay.

"You are with me in the dory – Manuel my name, and I come from schooner *We're Here* of Gloucester. I live to Gloucester. By and by we get supper. Eh, wha-at?"

He seemed to have two pairs of hands of cast-iron, for, not content with blowing through a big conch-shell, he must needs stand up to it, swaying with the sway of the flat-bottomed dory, and send a grinding, thuttering shriek through the fog. How long this entertainment lasted, Harvey could not remember, for he lay back terrified at the sight of the smoking swells. He fancied he heard a gun and a horn and shouting. Something bigger than the dory, but quite as lively, loomed alongside. Several voices talked at once; he was dropped into a dark, heaving hole, where men in oilskins gave him a hot drink, and took off his clothes, and he fell asleep.

When he waked he listened for the first break-fast-bell on the steamer, wondering why his state-room had grown so small. Turning, he looked into a narrow triangular cave, lit by a lamp hung against a huge square beam. A three-cornered table within arm's reach ran from the angle of the bows to the foremast. At the after end, behind a well-used Plymouth stove, sat a boy about his own age, with a flat, red face and a pair of twink-ling grey eyes. He was dressed in a blue jersey and high rubber boots. Several pairs of the same sort of footwear, an old cap, and some worn-out woollen socks lay on the floor, and black and yellow oilskins swayed to and fro beside the bunks. The place was packed as full of smells as a bale is of cotton. The oilskins had a peculiarly thick flavour of their own which made a sort of background to the smells of fried fish, burnt grease, paint, pepper, and stale tobacco; but these, again, were all hooped together by one en-circling smell of ship and salt water. Harvey saw with disgust that there were no sheets on his bed-place. He was lying on a piece of dingy ticking full of lumps and nubbles. Then, too, the boat's motion was not that of a steamer. She was neither sliding nor rolling, but rather wriggling herself about in a silly, aimless way, like a colt at the end of a halter. Water-noises ran by close to his ear, and beams creaked and whined about him. All these things made him grunt despairingly and think of his mother.

FROM CHAPTER II

The shadow of the masts and rigging, with the never-furled riding-sail, rolled to and fro on the heaving deck in the moonlight; and the pile of fish by the stern shone like a dump of fluid silver. In the hold there were tramplings and rumblings where Disko Troop and Tom Platt moved among the salt-bins. Dan passed Harvey a pitchfork, and led him to the inboard end of the rough table, where Uncle Salters was drumming impatiently with a knife-haft. A tub of salt water lay at his feet.

"You pitch to dad an' Tom Platt down the hatch, an' take keer Uncle Salters don't cut yer eye out," said Dan, swinging himself into the hold. "I'll pass salt below."

Penn and Manuel stood knee-deep among cod in the pen, flourishing drawn knives. Long Jack, a basket at his feet and mittens on his hands, faced Uncle Salters at the table, and Harvey stared at the pitchfork and the tub.

"Hi!" shouted Manuel, stooping to the fish, and bringing one up with a finger under its gill and a finger in its eye. He laid it on the edge of the pen; the knife-blade glimmered with a sound of tearing, and the fish, slit from throat to vent, with a nick on either side of the neck, dropped at Long Jack's feet.

"Hi!" said Long Jack, with a scoop of his mittened hand. The cod's liver dropped in the basket. Another wrench and scoop sent the head and offal flying, and the empty fish slid across to Uncle Salters, who snorted fiercely. There was another sound of tearing, the backbone flew over the bulwarks, and the fish, headless, gutted, and open, splashed in the tub, sending the salt water into Harvey's astonished mouth. After the first

Harvey Cheyne in the sea – an illustration from the first chapter of Captains Courageous.

yell, the men were silent. The cod moved along as though they were alive, and long ere Harvey had ceased wondering at the miraculous dexterity of it all, the tub was full.

"Pitch!" grunted Uncle Salters, without turning his head, and Harvey pitched the fish by twos and threes down the hatch.

"Hi! Pitch 'em bunchy," shouted Dan. "Don't scatter! Uncle Salters is the best splitter in the fleet. Watch him mind his book!"

Indeed, it looked a little as though the round uncle were cutting magazine pages against time. Manuel's body, cramped over from the hips, stayed like a statue; but his long arms grabbed the fish without ceasing. Little Penn toiled valiantly, but it was easy to see he was weak. Once or twice Manuel found time to help him without breaking the chain of supplies, and once Manuel howled because he had caught his finger in a Frenchman's hook. These hooks are made of soft metal to be re-bent after use; but the cod very often get away with them and are hooked again elsewhere; and that is one of the many reasons why Gloucester boats despise the Frenchmen.

Down below, the rasping sound of rough salt rubbed on rough flesh sounded like the whirring of a grindstone – a steady undertune to the "click-nick" of the knives in the pen, the wrench and schloop of torn heads, dropped liver, and flying offal; the "caraah" of Uncle Salters's knife scooping away backbone; and the flap of wet, opened bodies falling into the tub.

FROM CHAPTER VII

Next day they fell in with more sails, all circling slowly from the east northerly towards the west. But just when they expected to make the shoals by The Virgin the fog shut down, and they anchored surrounded by the tinklings of invisible bells. There was not much fishing, but occasionally dory met dory in the fog and exchanged news.

That night, a little before dawn, Dan and Harvey, who had been sleeping most of the day, tumbled out to "hook" fried pies. There was no reason why they should not have taken them openly; but they tasted better so, and it made the cook angry. The heat and smell below drove them on deck with their plunder, and they found Disko at the bell, which he handed over to Harvey.

"Keep her goin'," said he. "I mistrust I hear somethin'. Ef it's anything, I'm best where I am so's to get at things."

It was a forlorn little jingle; the thick air seemed to pinch it off; and in the pauses Harvey heard the muffled shriek of a liner's siren, and he knew enough of the Banks to know what that meant. It came to him, with horrible distinctness, how a boy in a cherry-coloured jersey – he despised

fancy blazers now with all a fisherman's contempt – how an ignorant, rowdy boy had once said it would be "great" if a steamer ran down a fishing-boat. That boy had a state-room with a hot and cold bath, and spent ten minutes each morning picking over a gilt-edged bill of fare. And that same boy – no, his very much older brother – was up at four of the dim dawn in streaming, crackling oilskins, hammering, literally for the dear life, on a bell smaller than the steward's breakfast bell, while somewhere close at hand a thirty-foot steel stem was storming along at twenty miles an hour! The bitterest thought of all was that there were folks asleep in dry, upholstered cabins who would never learn that they had massacred a boat before breakfast. So Harvey rang the bell.

"Yes, they slow daown one turn o' their blame propeller," said Dan, applying himself to Manuel's conch, "fer to keep inside the law, an' thet's consolin' when we're all at the bottom. Hark to her! She's a bumper!"

"Aooo – whoooo – whupp!' went the siren. "Wingle – tingle – tink," went the bell. "Graaa – ouch!' went the conch, while sea and sky were all milled up in milky fog. Then Harvey felt that he was near a moving body, and found himself looking up and up at the wet edge of a cliff-like bow, leaping, it seemed, directly over the schooner. A jaunty little feather of water curled in front of it, and as it lifted it showed a long ladder of Roman numerals – XV. XVI. XVII. XVIII. and so forth – on a salmon-coloured, gleaming side. It tilted forward and downward with a heart-stilling "Ssssooo"; the leader disappeared; a line of brass-rimmed portholes flashed past; a jet of steam puffed in Harvey's helplessly uplifted hands; a spout of hot water roared along the rail of the We're Here, and the little schooner staggered and shook in a rush of screw-torn water, as a liner's stern vanished in the fog. Harvey got ready to faint or be sick, or both, when he heard a crack like a trunk thrown on a sidewalk, and, all small in his ear, a far-away telephone-like voice drawl-ing: "Heave to! You've sunk us!"

"Is it us?" he gasped.

"No! Boat out yonder. Ring! We're goin' to look," said Dan, running out a dory.

In half a minute all except Harvey, Penn, and the cook were over-side and away. Presently a schooner's stump-foremast snapped clean across, drifted past the bows. Then an empty green dory came by, knocking on the *We're Here*'s side, as though she wished to be taken in. Then followed something, face down, in a blue jersey, but – it was not the whole of a man. Penn changed colour and caught his breath with a click. Harvey pounded despairingly at the bell, for he feared they might be sunk at any minute, and he jumped at Dan's hail as the crew came back.

"The *Jennie Cushman*," said Dan hysterically, "cut clean in ha'af – graound up an' trompled on at thet! Not a quarter mile away. Dad's got the old man. There ain't any one else, an' – there was his son too. Oh, Harve, Harve, I can't stand it! I've seen – " He dropped his head on his arms and sobbed while the others dragged a grey-headed man aboard.

"What did you pick me up fer?" the stranger groaned. "Disko, what did you pick me up fer?"

Disko dropped a heavy hand on his shoulder, for the man's eyes were wild and his lips trembled as he stared at the silent crew. Then up and spoke Pennsylvania Pratt, who was also Haskins or Rich or M'Vitty when Uncle Salters forgot; and his face was changed on him from the face of a fool to the countenance of an old, wise man, and he said in a strong voice: "The Lord gave, and the Lord hath taken away. Blessed be the name of the Lord!"

Excerpts from The Jungle Book

A "man's cub", escaping from a tiger, finds a home in a wolves' cave. Ambushing the tiger. The fight between the mongoose, Rikki-tikki-tavi, and the snake. The dance of the elephants.

FROM *MOWGLI'S BROTHERS*

It was seven o'clock of a very warm evening in the Seeonee hills when Father Wolf woke up from his day's rest, scratched himself, yawned, and spread out his paws one after the other to get rid of the sleepy feeling in their tips. Mother Wolf lay with her big gray nose dropped across her four tum-bling, squealing cubs, and the moon shone into the mouth of the cave where they all lived. "Augrh!" said Father Wolf, "it is time to hunt again"; and he was going to spring down hill when a little shadow with a bushy tail crossed the threshold and whined: "Good luck go with you, O Chief of the Wolves; and good luck and strong white teeth go with the noble children, that they may never forget the hungry in this world."

It was the jackal – Tabaqui, the Dish-licker – and the wolves of India despise Tabaqui because he runs about making mischief, and telling tales, and eating rags and pieces of leather from the village rubbish-heaps. But they are afraid of him too, because Tabaqui, more than any one else in the jungle, is apt to go mad, and then he forgets that he was ever afraid of any one, and runs through the forest biting everything in his way. Even the tiger runs and hides when little Tabaqui goes mad, for madness is the most disgraceful thing that can overtake a wild creature. We call it hydrophobia, but they call it *dewanee* – the madness - and run.

"Enter, then, and look," said Father Wolf, stiffly; "but there is no food here."

"For a wolf, no," said Tabaqui; "but for so mean a person as myself a dry bone is a good feast. Who are we, the Gidur-log (the jackal-people), to pick and choose?" He scuttled to the back of the cave, where he found the bone of a buck with some meat on it, and sat cracking the end merrily.

"All thanks for this good meal," he said, licking his lips. "How beautiful are the noble children! How large are their eyes! And so young too! Indeed, indeed, I might have remembered that the children of Kings are men from the beginning."

Now, Tabaqui knew as well as any one else that there is nothing so unlucky as to compliment children to their faces; and it pleased him to see Mother and Father Wolf look uncomfortable.

Tabaqui sat still, rejoicing in the mischief that he had made; then he said spitefully:

"Shere Khan, the Big One, has shifted his hunting-grounds. He will hunt among these hills for the next moon, so he has told me."

Shere Khan was the tiger who lived near the Waingunga River, twenty miles away.

"He has no right!" Father Wolf began angrily – "By the Law of the Jungle he has no right to change his quarters without due warning. He will frighten every head of game within ten miles, and I – I have to kill for two, these days."

"His mother did not call him Lungri (the Lame One) for nothing," said Mother Wolf, quietly. "He has been lame in one foot from his birth. That is why he has only killed cattle. Now the villagers of the Waingunga are angry with him, and he has come here to make *our* villagers angry. They will scour the jungle for him when he is far away, and we and our children must run when the grass is set alight. Indeed, we are very grateful to Shere Khan!"

"Shall I tell him of your gratitude?" said Tabaqui.

"Out!" snapped Father Wolf. "Out and hunt with thy master. Thou hast done harm enough for one night."

"I go," said Tabaqui quietly. "Ye can hear Shere Khan below in the thickets. I might have saved myself the message."

Father Wolf listened, and below in the valley that ran down to a little river, he heard the dry, angry, snarly, singsong whine of a tiger who has caught nothing and does not care if all the jungle knows it.

"The fool!" said Father Wolf. "To begin a night's work with that noise! Does he think that our buck are like his fat Waingunga bullocks?"

"H'sh! It is neither bullock nor buck he hunts to-night," said Mother Wolf. "It is Man." The whine had changed to a sort of humming purr that seemed to come from every quarter of the compass. It was the noise that bewilders woodcutters and gipsies sleeping in the open, and makes them run sometimes into the very mouth of the tiger.

"Man!" said Father Wolf, showing all his white teeth. "Faugh! Are there not enough beetles and frogs in the tanks that he must eat Man, and on our ground too!"

The Law of the Jungle, which never orders anything without a reason, forbids every beast to eat Man except when he is killing to show his children how to kill, and then he must hunt outside the hunting-grounds of his pack or tribe. The real reason for this is that man-killing means, sooner or later, the arrival of white men on elephants, with guns, and hundreds of brown men with gongs and rockets and torches. Then everybody in the jungle suffers. The reason the beasts give among themselves is that Man is the weakest and most defenceless of all living things, and it is unsportsmanlike to touch him. They say too – and it is true – that man-eaters become mangy, and lose their teeth.

The purr grew louder, and ended in the full-throated "Aaarh!" of the tiger's charge.

Then there was a howl – an untigerish howl – from Shere Khan. "He has missed," said Mother Wolf. "What is it?"

Father Wolf ran out a few paces and heard Shere Khan muttering and mumbling savagely, as he tumbled about in the scrub.

"The fool has had no more sense than to jump at a woodcutter's camp-fire, and has burned his feet," said Father Wolf, with a grunt. "Tabaqui is with him."

"Something is coming up hill," said Mother Wolf, twitching one ear. "Get ready."

The bushes rustled a little in the thicket, and Father Wolf dropped with his haunches under him, ready for his leap. Then, if you had been watching, you would have seen the most wonderful thing in the world – the wolf checked in mid-spring. He made his bound before he saw what it was he was jumping at, and then he tried to stop himself. The result was that he shot up straight into the air for four or five feet, landing almost where he left ground.

"Man!" he snapped. "A man's cub. Look!"

Directly in front of him, holding on by a low branch, stood a naked brown baby who could just walk – as soft and as dimpled a little atom as ever came to a wolf's cave at night. He looked up into Father Wolf's face, and laughed.

"Is that a man's cub?" said Mother Wolf. "I have never seen one. Bring it here."

A wolf accustomed to moving his own cubs can, if necessary, mouth an egg without breaking it, and though Father Wolf's jaws closed right on the child's back not a tooth even scratched the skin, as he laid it down among the cubs.

"How little! How naked and – how bold!" said Mother Wolf, softly. The baby was pushing his way between the cubs to get close to the warm hide. "Ahai! He is taking his meal with the others. And so this is a man's cub. Now, was there ever a wolf that could boast of a man's cub among her children?"

"I have heard now and again of such a thing, but never in our Pack or in my time," said Father Wolf. "He is altogether without hair, and I could kill him with a touch of my foot. But see, he looks up and is not afraid."

The moonlight was blocked out of the mouth of the cave, for Shere Khan's great square head and shoulders were thrust into the entrance. Tabaqui, behind him, was squeaking: "My lord, my lord, it went in here!"

"Shere Khan does us great honour," said Father Wolf, but his eyes were very angry. "What does Shere Khan need?"

"My quarry. A man's cub went this way," said Shere Khan. "Its parents have run off. Give it to me."

Shere Khan had jumped at a woodcutter's camp-fire, as Father Wolf had said, and was furious from the pain of his burned feet. But Father Wolf knew that the mouth of the cave was too narrow for a tiger to come in by. Even where he was, Shere Khan's shoulders and fore paws were cramped for want of room, as a man's would be if he tried to fight in a barrel.

"The Wolves are a free people," said Father Wolf. "They take orders from the Head of the Pack, and not from any striped cattle-killer. The man's cub is ours – to kill if we choose."

"Ye choose and ye do not choose! What talk is this of choosing? By the bull that I killed, am I to stand nosing into your dog's den for my fair dues? It is I, Shere Khan, who speak!"

The tiger's roar filled the cave with thunder. Mother Wolf shook herself clear of the cubs and sprang forward, her eyes, like two green moons in the darkness, facing the blazing eyes of Shere Khan.

"And it is I, Raksha (The Demon), who answer. The man's cub is mine, Lungri – mine to me! He shall not be killed. He shall live to run with the Pack and to hunt with the Pack; and in the end, look you, hunter of little naked cubs – frog-eater – fish-killer – he shall hunt *thee*! Now get hence, or

Harvey Cheyne and Captain Disko – from chapter two of Captains Courageous.

come in the end, O bush-tailed thieves!''

Mother Wolf threw herself down panting among the cubs, and Father Wolf said to her gravely:

''Shere Khan speaks this much truth. The cub must be shown to the Pack. Wilt thou still keep him, Mother?''

''Keep him!'' she gasped. ''He came naked, by night, alone and very hungry; yet he was not afraid! Look, he has pushed one of my babes to one side already. And that lame butcher would have killed him and would have run off to the Waingunga while the villagers here hunted through all our lairs in revenge! Keep him? Assuredly I will keep him. Lie still, little frog. O thou Mowgli – for Mowgli the Frog I will call thee – the time will come when thou wilt hunt Shere Khan as he has hunted thee.''

HUNTING-SONG OF THE SEEONEE PACK

As the dawn was breaking the Sambhur belled
    One, twice and again!
And a doe leaped up, and a doe leaped up
From the pond in the wood where the wild deer sup.
This I, scouting alone, beheld,
    One, twice and again!

As the dawn was breaking the Sambhur belled
    Once, twice and again!
And a wolf stole back, and a wolf stole back
To carry the word to the waiting pack,
And we sought and we found and we bayed on his track
    Once, twice and again!

As the dawn was breaking the Wolf Pack yelled
    Once, twice and again!
Feet in the jungle that leave no mark!
Eyes that can see in the dark – the dark!
Tongue – give tongue to it! Hark! O hark!
    Once, twice and again!

by the Sambhur that I killed (*I* eat no starved cattle), back thou goest to thy mother, burned beast of the jungle, lamer than ever thou comest into the world! Go!''

Father Wolf looked on amazed. He had almost forgotten the days when he won Mother Wolf in fair fight from five other wolves, when she ran in the Pack and was not called The Demon for compliment's sake. Shere Khan might have faced Father Wolf, but he could not stand up against Mother Wolf, for he knew that where he was she had all the advantage of the ground, and would fight to the death. So he backed out of the cave-mouth growling, and when he was clear he shouted:

''Each dog barks in his own yard! We will see what the Pack will say to this fostering of man-cubs. The cub is mine, and to my teeth he will

FROM *TIGER! TIGER!*

Herding in India is one of the laziest things in the world. The cattle move and crunch, and lie down, and move on again, and they do not even low. They only grunt, and the buffaloes very seldom say anything, but get down into the muddy pools one after another, and work their way into the mud till only their noses and staring china-blue eyes show above the surface, and there they lie like logs. The sun makes the rocks dance in the heat, and the herd-children hear one kite (never any more) whistling almost out of sight overhead, and they know that if they died, or a cow died, that kite would sweep down, and the next kite miles away would see him drop and would follow, and the next, and the next, and almost before they were dead there would be a score of hungry kites come out of nowhere. Then they sleep and wake and sleep again, and weave little baskets of dried grass and put grasshoppers in them; or catch two praying-mantises and make them fight; or string a necklace of red and black jungle-nuts; or watch a lizard basking on a rock, or a snake hunting a frog near the wallows. Then they sing long, long songs with odd native quavers at the end of them, and the day seems longer than most people's whole lives, and perhaps they make a mud castle with mud figures of men and horses and buffaloes, and put reeds into the men's hands, and pretend that they are kings and the figures are their armies, or that they are gods to be worshipped. Then evening comes, and the children call, and the buffaloes lumber up out of the sticky mud with noises like gunshots going off one after the other, and they all string across the gray plain back to the twinkling village lights.

Day after day Mowgli would lead the buffaloes out to their wallows, and day after day he would see Grey Brother's back a mile and a half away across the plain (so he knew that Shere Khan had not come back), and day after day he would lie on the grass listening to the noises round him, and dreaming of the old days in the jungle. If Shere Khan had made a false step with his lame paw up in the jungles by the Waingunga, Mowgli would have heard him in those long, still mornings.

At last a day came when he did not see Grey Brother at the signal-place, and he laughed and headed the buffaloes for the ravine by the *dhâk-tree*, which was all covered with golden-red flowers. There sat Grey Brother, every bristle on his back lifted.

"He has hidden for a month to throw thee off thy guard. He crossed the ranges last night with Tabaqui, hot-foot on thy trail," said the wolf, panting.

Mowgli frowned. "I am not afraid of Shere Khan, but Tabaqui is very cunning."

"Have no fear," said Grey Brother, licking his lips a little. "I met Tabaqui in the dawn. Now he is telling all his wisdom to the kites, but he told *me* everything before I broke his back. Shere Khan's plan is to wait for thee at the village gate this evening – for thee and for no one else. He is lying up now in the big dry ravine of the Waingunga."

"Has he eaten to-day, or does he hunt empty?" said Mowgli, for the answer meant life or death to him.

"He killed at dawn – a pig – and he has drunk too. Remember, Shere Khan could never fast, even for the sake of revenge."

"Oh! Fool, fool! What a cub's cub it is! Eaten and drunk too, and he thinks that I shall wait till he has slept! Now, where does he lie up? If there were but ten of us we might pull him down as he lies. These buffaloes will not charge unless they wind him, and I cannot speak their language. Can we get behind his track so that they may smell it?"

"He swam far down the Waingunga to cut that off," said Grey Brother.

"Tabaqui told him that, I know. He would

70

never have thought of it alone." Mowgli stood with his finger in his mouth, thinking. "The big ravine of the Waingunga. That opens out on the plain not half a mile from here. I can take the herd round through the jungle to the head of the ravine and then sweep down – but he would slink out at the foot. We must block that end. Grey Brother, canst thou cut the herd in two for me?"

"Not I, perhaps – but I have brought a wise helper." Grey Brother trotted off and dropped into a hole. Then there lifted up a huge gray head that Mowgli knew well, and the hot air was filled with the most desolate cry of all the jungle – the hunting-howl of a wolf at mid-day.

"Akela! Akela!" said Mowgli, clapping his hands. "I might have known that thou wouldst not forget me. We have a big work in hand. Cut the herd in two, Akela. Keep the cows and calves together, and the bulls and the plough-buffaloes by themselves."

The two wolves ran, ladies'-chain fashion, in and out of the herd, which snorted and threw up its head, and separated into two clumps. In one the cow-buffaloes stood, with their calves in the centre, and glared and pawed, ready, if a wolf would only stay still, to charge down and trample the life out of him. In the other the bulls and the young bulls snorted and stamped; but, though they looked more imposing, they were much less dangerous, for they had no calves to protect. No six men could have divided the herd so neatly.

"What orders?" panted Akela. "They are trying to join again."

Mowgli slipped on to Rama's back. "Drive the bulls away to the left, Akela. Grey Brother, when we are gone, hold the cows together, and drive them into the foot of the ravine."

"How far?" said Grey Brother, panting and snapping.

"Till the sides are higher than Shere Khan can jump," shouted Mowgli. "Keep them there till we come down." The bulls swept off as Akela bayed, and Grey Brother stopped in front of the cows. They charged down on him, and he ran just before them to the foot of the ravine, as Akela drove the bulls far to the left.

"Well done! Another charge and they are fairly started. Careful, now – careful, Akela. A snap too much, and the bulls will charge. *Huyah!* This is wilder work than driving black-buck. Didst thou think these creatures could move so swiftly?" Mowgli called.

"I have – hunted these too in my time," gasped Akela in the dust. "Shall I turn them into the jungle?"

"Ay, turn! Swiftly turn them! Rama is mad with rage. Oh, If I could only tell him what I need of him to-day!"

The bulls were turned to the right this time, and crashed into the standing thicket. The other herd-children, watching with the cattle half a mile away, hurried to the village as fast as their legs could carry them, crying that the buffaloes had gone mad and run away.

But Mowgli's plan was simple enough. All he wanted to do was to make a big circle uphill and get at the head of the ravine, and then take the bulls down it and catch Shere Khan between the bulls and the cows; for he knew that after a meal and a full drink Shere Khan would not be in any condition to fight or to clamber up the sides of the ravine. He was soothing the buffaloes now by voice, and Akela had dropped far to the rear, only whimpering once or twice to hurry the rear-guard. It was a long, long circle, for they did not wish to get too near the ravine and give Shere Khan warning. At last Mowgli rounded up the bewildered herd at the head of the ravine on a grassy patch that sloped steeply down to the ravine itself. From that height you could see across the tops of the trees down to the plain below; but what Mowgli looked at was the sides of the ravine, and he saw with a great deal of satisfaction that they ran nearly straight up and down, while the vines and creepers that hung over them would give no foothold to a tiger who wanted to get out.

"Let them breathe, Akela," he said, holding up his hand. "They have not winded him yet. Let them breathe. I must tell Shere Khan who comes. We have him in the trap."

He put his hands to his mouth and shouted down the ravine – it was almost like shouting down a tunnel – and the echoes jumped from rock to rock.

After a long time there came back the drawling, sleepy snarl of a full-fed tiger just wakened.

"Who calls?" said Shere Khan, and a splendid peacock fluttered up out of the ravine screeching.

"I, Mowgli. Cattle thief, it is time to come to the Council Rock! Down – hurry them down, Akela! Down, Rama, down!"

The herd paused for an instant at the edge of the slope, but Akela gave tongue in the full hunting-yell, and they pitched over one after the other, just as steamers shoot rapids, the sand and stones spurting up round them. Once started, there was no chance of stopping, and before they were fairly in the bed of the ravine Rama winded Shere Khan and bellowed.

"Ha! Ha!" said Mowgli, on his back. "Now thou knowest!" and the torrent of black horns, foaming muzzles, and staring eyes whirled down the ravine like boulders in flood-time; the weaker buffaloes being shouldered out to the sides of the ravine, where they tore through the creepers. They knew what the business was before them – the terrible charge of the buffalo-herd, against which no tiger can hope to stand. Shere Khan heard the thunder of their hoofs, picked himself up, and lumbered down the ravine, looking from side to side for some way of escape; but the walls of the ravine were straight, and he had to keep on, heavy with his dinner and his drink, willing to do anything rather than fight. The herd splashed through the pool he had just left, bellowing till the narrow cut rang. Mowgli heard an answering bellow from the foot of the ravine, saw Shere Khan turn (the tiger knew if the worst came to the worst it was better to meet the bulls than the cows with their calves), and then Rama tripped, stumbled, and went on again over something soft, and, with the bulls at his heels, crashed full into the other herd, while the weaker buffaloes were lifted clean off their feet by the shock of the meeting. That charge carried both herds out into the plain, goring and stamping and snorting. Mowgli watched his time, and slipped off Rama's neck, laying about him right and left with his stick.

"Quick, Akela! Break them up. Scatter them, or they will be fighting one another. Drive them away, Akela. *Hai*, Rama! *Hai! hai! hai!* my children. Softly now, softly! It is all over."

Akela and Grey Brother ran to and fro nipping the buffaloes' legs, and though the herd wheeled once to charge up the ravine again, Mowgli managed to turn Rama, and the others followed him to the wallows.

Shere Khan needed no more trampling. He was dead, and the kites were coming for him already.

"Brothers, that was a dog's death," said Mowgli, feeling for the knife he always carried in a sheath round his neck now that he lived with men. "But he would never have shown fight. His hide will look well on the Council Rock. We must get to work swiftly."

FROM *RIKKI-TIKKI-TAVI*

If you read the old books of natural history, you will find they say that when the mongoose fights the snake and happens to get bitten, he runs off and eats some herb that cures him. That is not true. The victory is only a matter of quickness of eye and quickness of foot – snake's blow against mongoose's jump – and as no eye can follow the motion of a snake's head when it strikes, that makes things much more wonderful than any magic herb. Rikki-tikki knew he was a young mongoose, and it made him all the more pleased to think that he had managed to escape a blow from behind. It gave him confidence in himself, and when Teddy came running down the path, Rikki-tikki was ready to be petted.

But just as Teddy was stooping, something flinched a little in the dust, and a tiny voice said: "Be careful. I am death!" It was Karait, the dusty brown snakeling that lies for choice on the dusty earth; and his bite is as dangerous as the cobra's. But he is so small that nobody thinks of him, and so he does the more harm to people.

Rikki-tikki's eyes grew red again, and he danced up to Karait with the peculiar rocking, swaying motion that he had inherited from his family. It looks funny, but it is so perfectly balanced a gait that you can fly off from it at any angle you please: and in dealing with snakes this is an advantage. If Rikki-tikki had only known, he was doing a much more dangerous thing than fighting Nag, for Karait is so small, and can turn so quickly, that unless Rikki bit him close to the back of the head, he would get the return-stroke in his eye or lip. But Rikki did not know; his eyes were all red, and he rocked back and forth, looking for a good place to hold. Karait struck out. Rikki jumped sideways and tried to run in, but the wicked little dusty grey head lashed within a fraction of his shoulder, and he had to jump over the body, and the head followed his heels close.

Teddy shouted to the house: "Oh, look here! Our mongoose is killing a snake"; and Rikki-tikki heard a scream from Teddy's mother. His father ran out with a stick, but by the time he came up, Karait had lunged out once too far, and Rikki-tikki had sprung, jumped on the snake's back, dropped his head far between his forelegs, bitten as high up the back as he could get hold, and rolled away. That bite paralysed Karait, and Rikki-tikki was just going to eat him up from the tail, after the custom of his family at dinner, when he remembered that a full meal makes a slow mongoose, and if he wanted all his strength and quickness ready, he must keep himself thin.

He went away for a dust-bath under the castor-oil bushes, while Teddy's father beat the dead Karait. "What is the use of that?" thought Rikki-tikki. "I have settled it all"; and then Teddy's mother picked him up from the dust and hugged him, crying that he had saved Teddy from death, and Teddy's father said that he was a providence, and Teddy looked on with big scared eyes. Rikki-tikki was rather amused at all the fuss, which, of course, he did not understand. Teddy's mother might just as well have petted Teddy for playing in the dust. Rikki was thoroughly enjoying himself.

That night, at dinner, walking to and fro among the wine-glasses on the table, he could have stuffed himself three times over with nice things; but he remembered Nag and Nagaina, and though it was very pleasant to be patted and petted by Teddy's mother, and to sit on Teddy's shoulder, his eyes would get red from time to time, and he would go off into his long war-cry of *"Rikk-tikk-tikki-tikki-tchk!"*

Teddy carried him off to bed, and insisted on Rikki-tikki sleeping under his chin. Rikki-tikki was too well bred to bite or scratch, but as soon as Teddy was asleep he went off for his nightly walk round the house, and in the dark he ran up against Chuchundra, the musk-rat, creeping round by the wall. Chuchundra is a broken-hearted little beast. He whimpers and cheeps all the night, trying to make up his mind to run into the middle of the room, but he never gets there.

"Don't kill me," said Chuchundra, almost weeping. "Rikki-tikki, don't kill me."

"Do you think a snake-killer kills musk-rats?" said Rikki-tikki scornfully.

"Those who kill snakes get killed by snakes,"

Mowgli's "brothers", an 1894 illustration for The Jungle Book.

said Chuchundra, more sorrowfully than ever. "And how am I to be sure that Nag won't mistake me for you some dark night?"

"There's not the least danger," said Rikki-tikki; "but Nag is in the garden, and I know you don't go there."

"My cousin Chua, the rat, told me –" said Chuchundra, and then he stopped.

"Told you what?"

"H'sh! Nag is everywhere, Rikki-tikki. You should have talked to Chua in the garden."

"I didn't – so you must tell me. Quick, Chuchundra, or I'll bite you!"

Chuchundra sat down and cried till the tears rolled off his whiskers. "I am a very poor man," he sobbed. "I never had spirit enough to run out into the middle of the room. H'sh! I mustn't tell you anything. Can't you *hear*, Rikki-tikki?"

Rikki-tikki listened. The house was as still as still, but he thought he could just catch the faintest *scratch-scratch* in the world – a noise as faint as that of a wasp walking on a window-pane – the dry scratch of a snake's scales on brick-work.

"That's Nag or Nagaina," he said to himself; "and he is crawling into the bath-room sluice. You're right, Chuchundra; I should have talked to Chua."

He stole off to Teddy's bath-room, but there was nothing there, and then to Teddy's mother's bath-room. At the bottom of the smooth plaster wall there was a brick pulled out to make a sluice for the bath-water, and as Rikki-tikki stole in by the masonry curb where the bath is put, he heard Nag and Nagaina whispering together outside in the moonlight.

"When the house is emptied of people," said Nagaina to her husband, "*he* will have to go away, and then the garden will be our own again. Go in quietly, and remember that the big man who killed Karait is the first one to bite. Then come out and tell me, and we will hunt for Rikki-tikki together."

"But are you sure that there is anything to be gained by killing the people?" said Nag.

"Everything. When there were no people in the bungalow, did we have any mongoose in the garden? So long as the bungalow is empty, we are king and queen of the garden; and remember that as soon as our eggs in the melon-bed hatch (as they may to-morrow), our children will need room and quiet."

"I had not thought of that," said Nag. "I will go, but there is no need that we should hunt for Rikki-tikki afterward. I will kill the big man and his wife, and the child if I can, and come away quietly. Then the bungalow will be empty, and Rikki-tikki will go."

Rikki-tikki tingled all over with rage and hatred at this, and then Nag's head came through the sluice, and his five feet of cold body followed it. Angry as he was, Rikki-tikki was very frightened as he saw the size of the big cobra. Nag coiled himself up, raised his head, and looked into the bath-room in the dark, and Rikki could see his eyes glitter.

"Now, if I kill him here, Nagaina will know; and if I fight him on the open floor, the odds are in his favour. What am I to do?" said Rikki-tikki-tavi.

Nag waved to and fro, and then Rikki-tikki heard him drinking from the biggest water-jar that was used to fill the bath. "That is good," said the snake. "Now, when Karait was killed, the big man had a stick. He may have that stick still, but when he comes in to bathe in the morning he will not have a stick. I shall wait here till he comes. Nagaina – do you hear me? – I shall wait here in the cool till daytime."

There was no answer from outside, so Rikki-tikki knew Nagaina had gone away. Nag coiled himself down, coil by coil, round the bulge at the bottom of the water-jar, and Rikki-tikki stayed still as death. After an hour he began to move, muscle by muscle, toward the jar. Nag was asleep, and Rikki-tikki looked at his big back, wondering which would be the best place for a good hold. "If I don't break his back at the first jump," said Rikki, "he can still fight; and if he fights – O Rikki!" He looked at the thickness of the neck below the hood, but that was too much for him; and a bite near the tail would only make Nag savage.

"It must be the head," he said at last; "the head above the hood; and when I am once there, I must not let go."

Then he jumped. The head was lying a little clear of the water-jar, under the curve of it; and, as his teeth met, Rikki braced his back against the bulge of the red earthenware to hold down the head. This gave him just one second's purchase, and he made the most of it. Then he was battered to and fro as a rat is shaken by a dog – to and fro on the floor, up and down, and round in great circles; but his eyes were red, and he held on as the body cart-whipped over the floor, upsetting the tin dipper and the soap-dish and the flesh-brush, and banged against the tin side of the bath. As he held he closed his jaws tighter and tighter, for he made sure he would be banged to death, and, for the honour of his family, he preferred to be found with his teeth locked. He was dizzy,

aching, and felt shaken to pieces when something went off like a thunderclap just behind him; a hot wind knocked him senseless, and red fire singed his fur. The big man had been wakened by the noise, and had fired both barrels of a shot-gun into Nag just behind the hood.

Rikki-tikki held on with his eyes shut, for now he was quite sure he was dead; but the head did not move, and the big man picked him up and said: "It's the mongoose again, Alice; the little chap has saved *our* lives now." Then Teddy's mother came in with a very white face, and saw what was left of Nag, and Rikki-tikki dragged himself to Teddy's bedroom and spent half the rest of the night shaking himself tenderly to find out whether he really was broken into forty pieces, as he fancied.

When morning came he was very stiff, but well pleased with his doings.

FROM *TOOMAI OF THE ELEPHANTS*

At last there was no sound of any more elephants moving in the forest, and Kala Nag rolled out from his station between the trees and went into the middle of the crowd, clucking and gurgling, and all the elephants began to talk in their own tongue, and to move about.

Still lying down, Little Toomai looked down upon scores and scores of broad backs, and wagging ears, and tossing trunks, and little rolling eyes. He heard the click of tusks as they crossed other tusks by accident, and the dry rustle of trunks twined together, and the chafing of enormous sides and shoulders in the crowd, and the incessant flick and *hissh* of the great tails. Then a cloud came over the moon, and he sat in black darkness; but the quiet, steady hustling and pushing and gurgling went on just the same. He knew that there were elephants all round Kala Nag, and that there was no chance of backing him out of the assembly; so he set his teeth and shivered. In a Keddah at least there was torch-light and shouting, but here he was all alone in the dark, and once a trunk came up and touched him on the knee.

Then an elephant trumpeted, and they all took it up for five or ten terrible seconds. The dew from the trees above spattered down like rain on the unseen backs, and a dull booming noise began, not very loud at first, and Little Toomai could not tell what it was; but it grew and grew, and Kala Nag lifted up one fore foot and then the other, and brought them down on the ground – one-two, one-two, as steadily as trip-hammers. The eleph-ants were stamping all together now, and it sounded like a war-drum beaten at the mouth of a cave. The dew fell from the trees till there was no more left to fall, and the booming went on, and the ground rocked and shivered, and Little Toomai put his hands up to his ears to shut out the sound. But it was all one gigantic jar that ran through him – this stamp of hundreds of heavy feet on the raw earth. Once or twice he could feel Kala Nag and all the others surge forward a few strides, and the thumping would change to the crushing sound of juicy green things being bruised, but in a minute or two the boom of feet on hard earth began again. A tree was creaking and groaning somewhere near him. He put out his arm and felt the bark, but Kala Nag moved forward, still tramping, and he could not tell where he was in the clearing. There was no sound from the elephants, except once, when two or three little calves squeaked together. Then he heard a thump and a shuffle, and the booming went on. It must have lasted fully two hours, and Little Toomai ached in every nerve; but he knew by the smell of the night air that the dawn was coming.

The morning broke in one sheet of pale yellow behind the green hills, and the booming stopped with the first ray, as though the light had been an order. Before Little Toomai had got the ringing out of his head, before even he had shifted his position, there was not an elephant in sight except Kala Nag, Pudmini, and the elephant with the rope-galls, and there was neither sign nor rustle nor whisper down the hillsides to show where the others had gone.

Little Toomai stared again and again. The clear-ing, as he remembered it, had grown in the night. More trees stood in the middle of it, but the under-growth and the jungle-grass at the sides had been rolled back. Little Toomai stared once more. Now he understood the trampling. The elephants had stamped out more room – had stamped the thick grass and juicy cane to trash, the trash into slivers, the slivers into tiny fibres, and the fibres into hard earth.

"Wah!" said Little Toomai, and his eyes were very heavy. "Kala Nag, my lord, let us keep by Pudmini and go to Petersen Sahib's camp, or I shall drop from thy neck."

The third elephant watched the two go away, snorted, wheeled round, and took his own path. He may have belonged to some little native king's establishment, fifty or sixty or a hundred miles away.

Two hours later, as Petersen Sahib was eating early breakfast, the elephants, who had been double-chained that night, began to trumpet, and Pudmini, mired to the shoulders, with Kala Nag, very foot-sore, shambled into the camp.

Little Toomai's face was grey and pinched, and his hair was full of leaves and drenched with dew; but he tried to salute Petersen Sahib, and cried faintly: "The dance – the elephant-dance! I have seen it, and – I die!" As Kala Nag sat down he slid off his neck in a dead faint.

But, since native children have no nerves worth speaking of, in two hours he was lying very con-tentedly in Petersen Sahib's hammock with Peter-sen Sahib's shooting-coat under his head, and a glass of warm milk, a little brandy, with a dash of quinine inside of him; and while the old hairy, scarred hunters of the jungle sat three-deep before him, looking at him as though he were a spirit, he told his tale in short words, as a child will, and wound up with:

"Now, if I lie in one word, send men to see, and they will find that the elephant-folk have trampled down more room in their dance-room, and they will find ten and ten, and many times ten, tracks leading to that dance-room. They made more room with their feet. I have seen it. Kala Nag took me, and I saw. Also Kala Nag is very leg-weary!"

Little Toomai lay back and slept all through the long afternoon and into the twilight, and while he slept Petersen Sahib and Machua Appa followed the track of the two elephants for fifteen miles across the hills. Petersen Sahib had spent eighteen years in catching elephants, and he had only once before found such a dance-place. Machua Appa had no need to look twice at the clearing to see what had been done there, or to scratch with his toe in the packed, rammed earth.

"The child speaks truth," said he. "All this was done last night, and I have counted seventy tracks crossing the river. See, Sahib, where Pudmini's leg-iron cut the bark off that tree! Yes; she was there too."

They looked at each other, and up and down, and they wondered; for the ways of elephants are beyond the wit of any man, black or white, to fathom.

"Forty years and five," said Machua Appa, "have I followed my lord, the elephant, but never have I heard that any child of man had seen what this child has seen. By all the Gods of the Hills, it is – what can we say?" and he shook his head.

When they got back to camp it was time for the evening meal. Petersen Sahib ate alone in his tent, but he gave orders that the camp should have two sheep and some fowls, as well as a double ration of flour and rice and salt, for he knew that there would be a feast.

Big Toomai had come up hot-foot from the camp in the plains to search for his son and his elephant, and now that he had found them he looked at them as though he were afraid of them both. And there was a feast by the blazing camp-fires in front of the lines of picketed elephants, and Little Toomai was the hero of it all; and the big brown elephant-catchers, the trackers and drivers and ropers, and the men who knew all the secrets of breaking the wildest elephants, passed him from one to the other, and they marked his forehead with blood from the breast of a newly killed jungle-cock, to show that he was a forester, initiated and free of all the jungles.

And at last, when the flames died down, and the red light of the logs made the elephants look as though they had been dipped in blood too, Machua Appa, the head of all the drivers of all the Keddahs – Machua Appa, Petersen Sahib's other self, who had never seen a made road in forty years: Machua Appa, who was so great that he had no other name than Machua Appa – leaped to his feet, with Little Toomai held high in the air above his head, and shouted: "Listen, my brothers. Listen, too, you my lords in the lines there, for I, Machua Appa, am speaking! This little one shall no more be called Little Toomai, but Toomai of the Elephants, as his great-grandfather was called before him. What never man has seen he has seen through the long night, and the favour of the elephant-folk and of the Gods of the Jungles is with him. He shall become a great tracker; he shall become greater than I, even I – Machua Appa! He shall follow the new trail, and the stale trail, with a clear eye! He shall take no harm in the Keddah when he runs under their bellies to rope the wild tuskers; and if he slips before the feet of the charging bull-elephant, that bull-elephant shall know who he is and shall not crush him. Aihai! my lords in the chains" – he whirled up the line of pickets – here is the little one that has seen your dances in your hidden places – the sight that never man saw! Give him honour, my lords! *Salaam karo*, my children. Make your salute to Toomai of the Elephants! Gunga Pershad, ahaa! Hira Guj, Birchi Guj, Kuttar Guj, ahaa! Pudmini – thou hast seen him at the dance, and thou too, Kala Nag, my pearl among elephants! – ahaa! Together! To Toomai of the Elephants. *Barrao!''*

And at that last wild yell the whole line flung up their trunks till the tips touched their foreheads, and broke out into the full salute, the crashing trumpet-peal that only the Viceroy of India hears – the Salaamut of the Keddah.

But it was all for the sake of Little Toomai, who had seen what never man had seen before – the dance of the elephants at night and alone in the heart of the Garo hills!

Excerpts from Kim

Kim, the young orphan of an Irish colour-sergeant, accompanies the old lama on his pilgrimage to the River of the Arrow.

FROM CHAPTER III

And they fared out from the gloom of the mango tope, the old man's high, shrill voice ringing across the field, as wail by long-drawn wail he unfolded the story of Nikal Seyn (Nicholson) – the song that men sing in the Punjab to this day. Kim was delighted, and the lama listened with deep interest.

"Ahi! Nikal Seyn is dead – he died before Delhi! Lances of the North, take vengeance for Nikal Seyn." He quavered it out to the end, marking the trills with the flat of his sword on the pony's rump.

"And now we come to the Big Road," said he, after receiving the compliments of Kim; for the lama was markedly silent. "It is long since I have ridden this way, but thy boy's talk stirred me. See, Holy One – the Great Road which is the backbone of all Hind. For the most part it is shaded, as here, with four lines of trees; the middle road – all hard – takes the quick traffic. In the days before rail-carriages the Sahibs travelled up and down here in hundreds. Now there are only country-carts and such-like. Left and right is the rougher road for the heavy carts – grain and cotton and timber, fodder, lime and hides. A man goes in safety here – for at every few *koss* is a police-station. The police are thieves and extortioners (I myself would patrol it with cavalry – young recruits under a strong captain), but at least they do not suffer any rivals. All castes and kinds of men move here. Look! Brahmins and chumars, bankers and tinkers, barbers and bun-nias, pilgrims and potters – all the world going and coming. It is to me as a river from which I am withdrawn like a log after a flood."

And truly the Grand Trunk Road is a wonderful spectacle. It runs straight, bearing without crowd-ing India's traffic for fifteen hundred miles – such a river of life as nowhere else exists in the world. They looked at the green-arched, shade-flecked length of it, the white breadth speckled with slow-pacing folk; and the two-roomed police-station opposite.

"Who bears arms against the law?" a constable called out laughingly, as he caught sight of the soldier's sword. "Are not the police enough to destroy evil-doers?"

"It was because of the police I bought it," was the answer. "Does all go well in Hind?"

"Rissaldar Sahib, all goes well."

"I am like an old tortoise, look you, who puts his head out from the bank and draws it in again. Ay, this is the Road of Hindustan. All men come by this way. . . ."

"Son of a swine, is the soft part of the road meant for thee to scratch thy back upon? Father of all the daughters of shame and husband of ten thousand virtueless ones, thy mother was devoted to a devil, being led thereto by her mother. Thy aunts have never had a nose for seven generations! Thy sister – What owl's folly told thee to draw thy carts across the road? A broken wheel? Then take a broken head and put the two together at leisure!"

The voice and the venomous whip-cracking came out of a pillar of dust fifty yards away, where a cart had broken down. A thin, high Kathiawar mare, with eyes and nostrils aflame, rocketed out of the jam, snorting and wincing as her rider bent her across the road in chase of a shouting man. He was tall and grey-bearded, sit-ting the almost mad beast as a piece of her, and scientifically lashing his victim between plunges.

The old man's face lit with pride. "My child!" said he briefly, and strove to rein the pony's neck to a fitting arch.

"Am I to be beaten before the police?" cried the carter. "Justice! I will have Justice – "

"Am I to be blocked by a shouting ape who upsets ten thousand sacks under a young horse's nose? That is the way to ruin a mare."

"He speaks truth. He speaks truth. But she follows her man close," said the old man. The carter ran under the wheels of his cart and thence threatened all sorts of vengeance.

"They are strong men, thy sons," said the policeman serenely, picking his teeth.

The horseman delivered one last vicious cut with his whip and came on at a canter.

"My father!" He reined back ten yards and dismounted.

The old man was off his pony in an instant, and they embraced as do father and son in the East.

FROM CHAPTER VIII

Kim will remember till he dies that long, lazy journey from Umballa, through Kalka and the Pin-jore Gardens near by, up to Simla. A sudden spate in the Gugger River swept down one horse (the most valuable, be sure), and nearly drowned Kim among the dancing boulders. Farther up the road horses were stampeded by a Government eleph-ant, and being in high condition of grass food, it cost a day and a half to get them together again. Then they met Sikandar Khan coming down with a few unsaleable screws – remnants of his string – and Mahbub, who has more of horse-coping in his little finger-nail than Sikandar Khan in all his tents, must needs buy two of the worst, and that meant eight hours' laborious diplomacy and un-told tobacco. But it was all pure delight – the wandering road, climbing, dipping, and sweeping about the growing spurs; the flush of the morning laid along the distant snows; the branched cacti, tier upon tier on the stony hillsides; the voices of a thousand water-channels; the chatter of the monkeys; the solemn deodars, climbing one after another with down-drooped branches; the vista of the Plains rolled out far beneath them; the incessant twanging of the tonga-horns and the wild rush of the led horses when a tonga swung round a curve; the halts for prayers (Mahbub was very religious in dry-washings and bellowings when time did not press); the evening conferences by the halting-places, when camels and bullocks chewed solemnly together and the stolid drivers told the news of the Road – all these things lifted Kim's heart to song within him.

Toomai of the Elephants, *an illustration by W. Strang (1899).*

"But, when the singing and dancing is done," said Mahbub Ali, "comes the Colonel Sahib's, and that is not so sweet."

"A fair land – a most beautiful land is this of Hind – and the land of the Five Rivers is fairer than all," Kim half chanted. "Into it I will go again if Mahbub Ali or the Colonel lift hand or foot against me. Once gone, who shall find me? Look, Hajji, is yonder the city of Simla? Allah, what a city!"

"My father's brother, and he was an old man Mackerson Sahib's well was new at Peshawar, could recall when there were but two houses in it."

He led the horses below the main road into the lower Simla bazar – the crowded rabbit-warren that climbs up from the valley to the Town Hall at an angle of forty-five. A man who knows his way there can defy all the police of India's summer capital, so cunningly does veranda communicate with veranda, alley-way with alley-way, and bolt-hole with bolt-hole. Here live those who minister to the wants of the glad city – *jhampanis* who pull the pretty ladies' rickshaws by night and gamble till the dawn; grocers, oil-sellers, curio-vendors, firewood-dealers, priests, pickpockets, and native employees of the Government. Here are discussed by courtesans the things which are supposed to be profoundest secrets of the India Council; and here gather all the sub-sub-agents of half the Native States. Here, too, Mahbub Ali rented a room, much more securely locked than his bulk-head at Lahore, in the house of a Mohammedan cattle-dealer. It was a place of miracles, too, for there went in at twilight a Mohammedan horse-boy, and there came out an hour later a Eurasian lad – the Lucknow girl's dye was of the best – in badly fitting shop-clothes.

"I have spoken with Creighton Sahib," quoth Mahbub Ali, "and a second time has the Hand of Friendship averted the Whip of Calamity. He says that thou hast altogether wasted sixty days upon the Road, and it is too late, therefore, to send thee to any Hill-school."

"I have said that my holidays are my own. I do not go to school twice over. That is one part of my bond."

"The Colonel Sahib is not yet aware of that contract. Thou art to lodge in Lurgan Sahib's house till it is time to go again to Nucklao."

"I had sooner lodge with thee, Mahbub."

"Thou dost not know the honour. Lurgan Sahib himself asked for thee. Thou wilt go up the hill and along the road atop, and there thou must forget for a while that thou hast ever seen or spoken to me, Mahbub Ali, who sells horses to Creighton Sahib, whom thou dost not know. Remember this order."

Kim nodded. "Good," said he, "and who is Lurgan Sahib? Nay" – he caught Mahbub's sword-keen glance – "indeed I have never heard his name. Is he by chance" – he lowered his voice – "one of us?"

"What talk is this of us, Sahib?" Mahbub Ali returned, in the tone he used towards Europeans. Lurgan Sahib has a shop among the European shops. All Simla knows it. Ask there . . . and, Friend of all the World, he is one to be obeyed to the last wink of his eyelashes. Men say he does magic, but that should not touch thee. Go up the hill and ask. Here begins the Great Game."

FROM CHAPTER XV

The lama held his peace. Except for the click of the rosary and a faint *clop-clop* of Mahbub's retreating feet, the soft, smoky silence of evening in India wrapped them close.

"Hear me! I bring news."

"But let us – "

Out shot the long yellow hand compelling silence. Kim tucked his feet under his robe-edge obediently.

"Hear me! I bring news! The Search is finished. Comes now the Reward. . . . Thus. When we were among the Hills, I lived on thy strength till the young branch bowed and nigh broke. When we came out of the Hills, I was troubled for thee and for other matters which I held in my heart. The boat of my soul lacked direction; I could not see into the Cause of Things. So I gave thee over to the virtuous woman altogether. I took no food. I

drank no water. Still I saw not the Way. They pressed food upon me and cried at my shut door. So I removed myself to a hollow under a tree. I took no food. I took no water. I sat in meditation two days and two nights, abstracting my mind; inbreathing and outbreathing in the required manner. . . . Upon the second night – so great was my reward – the wise Soul loosed itself from the silly Body, and went free. This I have never before attained, though I have stood on the threshold of it. Consider, for it is a marvel!"

"A marvel indeed. Two days and two nights without food! Where was the Sahiba?" said Kim under his breath.

"Yea, my Soul went free, and, wheeling like an eagle, saw indeed that there was no Teshoo Lama nor any other soul. As a drop draws to water, so my Soul drew near to the Great Soul which is beyond all things. At that point, exalted in contemplation, I saw all Hind, from Ceylon in the sea to the Hills, and my own Painted Rocks at Suchzen; I saw every camp and village, to the least, where we have ever rested. I saw them at one time and in one place; for they were within the Soul. By this I knew the Soul had passed beyond the illusion of Time and Space and of Things. By this I knew that I was free. I saw thee lying in thy cot, and I saw thee falling downhill under the idolater – at one time, in one place, in my Soul, which, as I say, had touched the Great Soul. Also I saw the stupid body of Teshoo Lama lying down, and the *hakim* from Dacca kneeled beside, shouting in its ear. Then my Soul was all alone, and I saw nothing, for I was all things, having reached the Great Soul. And I meditated a thousand thousand years, passionless, well aware of the Causes of all Things. Then a voice cried: "What shall come to the boy if thou art dead?" and I was shaken back and forth in myself with pity for thee; and I said: 'I will return to my *chela*, lest he miss the Way.' Upon this my Soul, which is the Soul of Teshoo Lama, withdrew itself from the

On the Grand Trunk, *a terracotta relief by John Kipling for the third chapter of* Kim *(1901)*.

Great Soul with strivings and yearnings and retchings and agonies not to be told. As the egg from the fish, as the fish from the water, as the water from the cloud, as the cloud from the thick air, so put forth, so leaped out, so drew away, so fumed up the Soul of Teshoo Lama from the Great Soul. Then a voice cried: 'The River! Take heed to the River!' and I looked down upon all the world, which was as I had seen it before – one in time, one in place – and I saw plainly the River of the Arrow at my feet. At that hour my Soul was hampered by some evil or other whereof I was not wholly cleansed, and it lay upon my arms and coiled round my waist; but I put it aside, and I cast forth as an eagle in my flight for the very place of the River. I pushed aside world upon world for thy sake. I saw the River below me – the River of the Arrow – and, descending, the waters of it closed over me; and behold I was again in the body of Teshoo Lama, but free from sin, and the *hakim* from Dacca bore up my head in the waters of the River. It is here! It is behind the mango-tope here – even here!''

''*Allah kerim!* Oh, well that the Babu was by! Wast thou very wet?''

''Why should I regard? I remember the *hakim* was concerned for the body of Teshoo Lama. He haled it out of the holy water in his hands, and there came afterwards thy horse-seller from the North with a cot and men, and they put the body on the cot and bore it up to the Sahiba's house.''

''What said the Sahiba?''

''I was meditating in that body, and did not hear. So thus the Search is ended. For the merit that I have acquired, the River of the Arrow is here. It broke forth at our feet, as I have said. I have found it. Son of my Soul, I have wrenched my Soul back from the Threshold of Freedom to free thee from all sin – as I am free, and sinless! Just is the Wheel! Certain is our deliverance! Come!''

He crossed his hands on his lap and smiled, as a man may who has won salvation for himself and his beloved.

Excerpt from Puck of Pook's Hill

Of all the pagan inhabitants of England, only one, Weland the smith, survived. Puck, the spirit of the hills, tells his story.

FROM *WELAND'S SWORD*

"They were always landing in those days, or being driven back to their ships, and they always brought their Gods with them. England is a bad country for Gods. Now, *I* began as I mean to go on. A bowl of porridge, a dish of milk, and a little quiet fun with the country folk in the lanes was enough for me then, as it is now. I belong here, you see, and I have been mixed up with people all my days. But most of the others insisted on being Gods, and having temples, and altars, and priests, and sacrifices of their own."

"People burned in wicker baskets?" said Dan. "Like Miss Blake tells us about?"

"All sorts of sacrifices," said Puck. "If it wasn't men, it was horses, or cattle, or pigs, or metheglin – that's a sticky, sweet sort of beer. *I* never liked it. They were a stiff-necked, extravagant set of idols, the Old Things. But what was the result? Men don't like being sacrificed at the best of times; they don't even like sacrificing their farm-horses. After a while, men simply left the Old Things alone, and the roofs of their temples fell in, and the Old Things had to scuttle out and pick up a living as they could. Some of them took to hanging about trees, and hiding in graves and groaning o' nights. If they groaned loud enough and long enough they might frighten a poor countryman into sacrificing a hen, or leaving a pound of butter for them. I remember one Goddess called Belisama. She became a common wet water-spirit somewhere in Lancashire. And there

were hundreds of other friends of mine. First they were Gods. Then they were People of the Hills, and then they flitted to other places because they couldn't get on with the English for one reason or another. There was only one Old Thing, I remember, who honestly worked for his living after he came down in the world. He was called Weland, and he was a smith to some Gods. I've forgotten their names, but he used to make them swords and spears. I think he claimed kin with Thor of the Scandinavians.

"*Heroes of Asgard* Thor?" said Una. She had been reading the book.

"Perhaps," answered Puck. "None the less, when bad times came, he didn't beg or steal. He worked; and I was lucky enough to be able to do him a good turn."

"Tell us about it," said Dan. "I think I like hearing of Old Things."

They rearranged themselves comfortably, each chewing a grass stem. Puck propped himself on one strong arm and went on:

"Let's think! I met Weland first on a November afternoon in a sleet storm, on Pevensey Level – "

"Pevensey? Over the hill, you mean?" Dan pointed south.

"Yes; but it was all marsh in those days, right up to Horsebridge and Hydeneye. I was on Beacon Hill – they called it Brunanburgh then – when I saw the pale flame that burning thatch makes, and I went down to look. Some pirates – I think they must have been Peofn's men – were burning a village on the Levels, and Weland's image – a big, black wooden thing with amber beads round his neck – lay in the bows of a black thirty-two-oar galley that they had just beached. Bitter cold it was! There were icicles hanging from her deck and the oars were glazed over with ice, and there was ice on Weland's lips. When he saw me he began a long chant in his own tongue, telling me how he was going to rule England, and how I should smell the smoke of his altars from

Lincolnshire to the Isle of Wight. *I* didn't care! I'd seen too many Gods charging into Old England to be upset about it. I let him sing himself out while his men were burning the village, and then I said (I don't know what put it into my head), 'Smith of the Gods,' I said, 'the time comes when I shall meet you plying your trade for hire by the wayside.'"

"What did Weland say?" said Una. "Was he angry?"

"He called me names and rolled his eyes, and I went away to wake up the people inland. But the pirates conquered the country, and for centuries Weland was a most important God. He had temples everywhere – from Lincolnshire to the Isle of Wight, as he said – and his sacrifices were simply scandalous. To do him justice, he preferred horses to men; but men *or* horses, I knew that presently he'd have to come down in the world – like the other Old Things. I gave him lots of time – I gave him about a thousand years – and at the end of 'em I went into one of his temples near Andover to see how he prospered. There was his altar, and there was his image, and there were his priests, and there were the congregation, and everybody seemed quite happy, except Weland and the priests. In the old days the congregation were unhappy until the priests had chosen their sacrifices; and so would *you* have been. When the service began a priest rushed out, dragged a man up to the altar, pretended to hit him on the head with a little gilt axe, and the man fell down and pretended to die. Then everybody shouted: 'A sacrifice to Weland! A sacrifice to Weland!'"

"And the man wasn't really dead?" said Una.

"Not a bit. All as much pretence as a dolls' tea-party. Then they brought out a splendid white horse, and the priest cut some hair from its mane and tail and burned it on the altar, shouting, 'A sacrifice!' That counted the same as if a man and a horse had been killed. I saw poor Weland's face through the smoke, and I couldn't help laughing.

He looked so disgusted and so hungry, and all he had to satisfy himself was a horrid smell of burning hair. Just a dolls' tea-party!"

"I judged it better not to say anything then ('twouldn't have been fair), and the next time I came to Andover, a few hundred years later, Weland and his temple were gone, and there was a Christian bishop in a church there. None of the People of the Hills could tell me anything about him, and I supposed that he had left England." Puck turned, lay on his other elbow, and thought for a long time.

"Let's see," he said at last. "It must have been some few years later – a year or two before the Conquest, I think – that I came back to Pook's Hill here, and one evening I heard old Hobden talking about Weland's Ford."

"If you mean old Hobden the hedger, he's only seventy-two. He told me so himself," said Dan. "He's an intimate friend of ours."

"You're quite right," Puck replied. "I meant old Hobden's ninth great-grandfather. He was a free man and burned charcoal hereabouts. I've known the family, father and son, so long that I get confused sometimes. Hob of the Dene was my Hobden's name, and he lived at the Forge cottage. Of course, I pricked up my ears when I heard Weland mentioned, and I scuttled through the woods to the Ford just beyond Bog Wood yonder." He jerked his head westward, where the valley narrows between wooded hills and steep hop-fields.

"Why, that's Willingford Bridge," said Una. "We go there for walks often. There's a kingfisher there."

"It was Weland's Ford then, dearie. A road led down from the Beacon on the top of the hill – a shocking bad road it was – and all the hillside was thick, thick oak-forest, with deer in it. There was no trace of Welland, but presently I saw a fat old farmer riding down from the Beacon under the greenwood tree. His horse had cast a shoe in the clay, and when he came to the Ford he dismounted, took a penny out of his purse, laid it on a stone, tied the old horse to an oak, and called out: 'Smith, Smith, here is work for you!' Then he sat down and went to sleep. You can imagine how *I* felt when I saw a white-bearded old blacksmith in a leather apron creep out from behind the oak and begin to shoe the horse. It was Weland himself. I was so astonished that I jumped out and said: 'What on Human Earth are you doing here, Weland?'"

"Poor Weland!" sighed Una.

"He pushed the long hair back from his forehead (he didn't recognise me at first). Then he said: '*You* ought to know. You foretold it, Old Thing. I'm shoeing horses for hire. I'm not even Weland now,' he said. 'They call me Wayland-Smith.'"

"Poor chap!" said Dan. "What did you say?"

"What could I say? He looked up, with the horse's foot on his lap, and he said, smiling, 'I remember the time when I wouldn't have accepted this old bag of bones as a sacrifice, and now I'm glad enough to shoe him for a penny.'

"'Isn't there any way for you to get back to Valhalla, or wherever you come from?' I said.

"'I'm afraid not,' he said, rasping away at the hoof. He had a wonderful touch with horses. The old beast was whinnying on his shoulder. 'You may remember that I was not a gentle God in my Day and my Time and my Power. I shall never be released till some human being truly wishes me well.'

"'Surely,' said I, 'the farmer can't do less than that. You're shoeing the horse all round for him.'

"'Yes,' said he, 'and my nails will hold a shoe from one full moon to the next. But farmers and Weald clay,' said he, 'are both uncommon cold and sour.'

"Would you believe it, that when that farmer woke and found his horse shod he rode away without one word of thanks? I was so angry that

I wheeled his horse right round and walked him back three miles to the Beacon, just to teach the old sinner politeness."

"Were you invisible?" said Una. Puck nodded, gravely.

"The Beacon was always laid in those days ready to light, in case the French landed at Pevensey; and I walked the horse about and about it that lee-long summer night. The farmer thought he was bewitched – well, he *was*, of course – and began to pray and shout. *I* didn't care! I was as good a Christian as he any fair-day in the County, and about four o'clock in the morning a young novice came along from the monastery that used to stand on the top of Beacon Hill."

"What's a novice?" said Dan.

"It really means a man who is beginning to be a monk, but in those days people sent their sons to a monastery just the same as a school. This young fellow had been to a monastery in France for a few months every year, and he was finishing his studies in the monastery close to his home here. Hugh was his name, and he had got up to go fishing hereabouts. His people owned all this valley. Hugh heard the farmer shouting, and asked him what in the world he meant. The old man spun him a wonderful tale about fairies and goblins and witches; and I *know* he hadn't seen a thing except rabbits and red deer all that night. (The People of the Hills are like otters – they don't show except when they choose.) But the novice wasn't a fool. He looked down at the horse's feet, and saw the new shoes fastened as only Weland knew how to fasten 'em. (Weland had a way of turning down the nails that folks called the Smith's Clinch.)

"'H'm!' said the novice. 'Where did you get your horse shod?'

"The farmer wouldn't tell him at first, because the priests never like their people to have any dealings with the Old Things. At last he confessed that the Smith had done it. 'What did you pay him?' said the novice. 'Penny,' said the farmer, very sulkily. 'That's less than a Christian would have charged,' said the novice. 'I hope you threw a "thank you" into the bargain.' 'No,' said the farmer; 'Wayland-Smith's a heathen.' 'Heathen or no heathen,' said the novice, 'you took his help, and where you get help there you must give thanks.' 'What?' said the farmer – he was in a furious temper because I was walking the old horse in circles all this time – 'What, you young jackanapes?' said he. 'Then by your reasoning I ought to say "thank you" to Satan if he helped me?' 'Don't roll about up there splitting reasons with me,' said the novice. 'Come back to the Ford and thank the Smith, or you'll be sorry.'

"Back the farmer had to go. I led the horse, though no one saw me, and the novice walked beside us, his gown swishing through the shiny dew and his fishing-rod across his shoulders, spear-wise. When we reached the Ford again – it was five o'clock and misty still under the oaks – the farmer simply wouldn't say 'thank you'. He said he'd tell the Abbot that the novice wanted him to worship heathen Gods. Then Hugh the novice lost his temper. He just cried 'Out!' put his arm under the farmer's fat leg, and heaved him from the saddle on to the turf, and before he could rise he caught him by the back of the neck and shook him like a rat till the farmer growled, 'Thank you, Wayland-Smith.' "

"Did Weland see all this?" said Dan.

"Oh yes, and he shouted his old war-cry when the farmer thudded on to the ground. He was delighted. Then the novice turned to the oak tree and said, 'Ho, Smith of the Gods! I am ashamed of this rude farmer; but for all you have done in kindness and charity to him and to others of our people, I thank you and wish you well.' Then he picked up his fishing-rod – it looked more like a tall spear than ever – and tramped off down the valley."

"And what did poor Weland do?" said Una.

"He laughed and he cried with joy, because he had been released at last, and could go away. But he was an honest Old Thing. He had worked for his living and he paid his debts before he left. 'I shall give that novice a gift,' said Weland. 'A gift that shall do him good the wide world over and Old England after him. Blow up my fire, Old Thing, while I get the iron for my last task.' Then he made a sword – a dark-grey, wavy-lined sword – and I blew the fire while he hammered. By Oak, Ash and Thorn, I cooled that sword in running water twice, and the third time he cooled it in the evening dew, and he laid it out in the moonlight and said Runes (that's charms) over it, and he carved Runes of Prophecy on the blade. 'Old Thing,' he said to me, wiping his forehead, 'this is the best blade that Weland ever made. Even the user will never know how good it is. Come to the monastery.'

"We went to the dormitory where the monks slept, we saw the novice fast asleep in his cot, and Weland put the sword into his hand, and I remember the young fellow gripped it in his sleep. Then Weland strode as far as he dared into the Chapel and threw down all his shoeing-tools – his hammers, his pincers, and rasps – to show that he had done with them for ever. It sounded like suits of armour falling, and the sleepy monks ran in, for they thought the monastery had been attacked by the French. The novice came first of all, waving his new sword and shouting Saxon battle-cries. When they saw the shoeing-tools they were very bewildered, till the novice asked leave to speak, and told what he had done to the farmer, and what he had said to Wayland-Smith, and how, though the dormitory light was burning, he had found the wonderful Rune-carved sword in his cot.

"The Abbot shook his head at first, and then he laughed and said to the novice: 'Son Hugh, it needed no sign from a heathen God to show me

Illustration by Arthur Rackham
for Weland's Sword *(1906).*

that you will never be a monk. Take your sword, and keep your sword, and go with your sword, and be as gentle as you are strong and courteous. We will hang up the Smith's tools before the Altar,' he said, 'because, whatever the Smith of the Gods may have been in the old days, we know that he worked honestly for his living and made gifts to Mother Church.' Then they went to bed again, all except the novice, and he sat up in the garth playing with his sword. Then Weland said to me by the stables: 'Farewell, Old Thing; you had the right of it. You saw me come to England, and you see me go. Farewell!' ''

Below: *The lama, by J. Lockwood Kipling, from Rudyard Kipling's masterpiece* Kim

Kipling's Characters

Kipling discovered his fictional characters in schools and streets, in bazaars, in barracks and on battlefields, on land and at sea.

The characters created by Kipling are legion and only a few of them can be described in detail here. Some of them, especially those that appear in the short stories, are no more than rough sketches, but even they, in the way they look or speak or behave, help to evoke the real and vivid atmosphere of a particular place and time – the colour and mystery of India, the rough cameraderie of an army barracks, the spartan discipline of an English public school, the peril and excitement of an ocean trawler. In a life spent largely in travel, full of strange encounters and unusual adventures, Kipling found his heroes in the most unlikely settings. Some are pure figments of his imagination but the majority spring from remembered experience. Few of them emerge as fully rounded characters with features sufficiently individualised as to represent the author himself at any stage of his career; at best they mirror fleeting thoughts and sensations – happy, sad, angry, cynical, optimistic, dream-like or mystical, depending on mood and circumstance. In short, they are fragmented projections of his inner self, personifications of his most passionate beliefs and hopes.

Any detailed analysis of Kipling's characters must therefore take into account the writer's personal attitudes, particularly his political "credo", formulated as it was by experiences in both East and West over a period of some fifty years. He persuaded himself that it was his responsibility to convey his cherished beliefs and opinions to as wide a public as possible, no matter whether disguised as fiction or plainly expressed in a newspaper article, political pamphlet or essay. This is a key to the understanding of Kipling's works and a clue to their limitations and shortcomings.

The characters best exemplifying the warm humanity of the writer are those based on happy memories of childhood and youth, before his political views and moral attitudes became too rigid and inflexible.

Dick Heldar and Torpenhow

The first really ambitious character to figure in Kipling's novels is Dick Heldar, the hero of *The Light that Failed*. He is the painter who, having achieved fame after a series of long and bitter experiences, is compelled to struggle against the terrible affliction of gradual blindness and eventually dies, never acknowledging that he is beaten, proud in human strength and dignity. In the first part of the story there can be little doubt that Dick represents Kipling himself as a boy, forced to part from his parents, complete his education in England and live with a harsh foster-mother. In the book she is Mrs Jennett, obviously modelled on the bible-thumping Aunty Rosa who had made the young Rudyard's life such a misery. This is how Kipling describes her: "Her religion, manufactured in the main by her own intelligence and a keen study of the Scriptures, was an aid to her in this matter. At such times as she herself was not personally displeased with Dick, she left him to understand that he had a heavy account to settle with his Creator; wherefore Dick learned to loathe his God as intensely as he loathed Mrs Jennett; and this is not a wholesome frame of mind for the young.... The treatment taught him at least the power of living alone – a power that was of service to him when he went to a public school and the boys laughed at his clothes, which were poor in quality and much mended."

Dick is engaged in a perpetual search for the love he is denied in childhood and for which a blind faith in God proves no substitute. He finds a sympathetic friend in Torpenhow, nicknamed Torp, a war correspondent whom he meets in Egypt during the Sudan campaign. This man, with whom he shares some dangerous moments, settles in a large room at the top of a house overlooking the Thames, finds work for the young painter, tries to console him when stricken by blindness and is close at hand when

Kipling at his desk, seated at the feet of his best-known characters (illustration by Cyrus Cunes).

he dies. There is much of Kipling in this portrait of a generous-hearted journalist who eagerly signs on as a war correspondent, careless of risk, motivated by a sense of adventure and concerned to report the truth as he sees it, no matter what the consequences.

As a war correspondent Kipling was often taken to task for exceeding his brief and not restricting himself to simple, dispassionate reporting of events. To modern readers many of his articles would certainly seem over-bombastic, but we have to remember the heady climate in which he was working and the effect he was aiming for. Conscious of being the only eye-witness capable of describing dramatic scenes of bravery and suffering to thousands of readers at home, a war correspondent was surely entitled to exercise a little artistic licence in order to convey the excitement and colour of the battlefield. Torp knows quite well that the Central Southern Syndicate for which he works is not really interested in military manoeuvres and broad plans of battle but is looking for picturesque material designed for mass circulation. The average reader, then as today, was more fascinated by a touching account of a courageous soldier leaving the ranks to rescue a wounded comrade than by a factual report of the deliberations of a group of elderly generals planning the next move of their campaign. Torpenhow therefore does not pull his punches, reproducing the rough, crude language of the troops just as Kipling himself did in his *Barrack-Room Ballads* and short stories of army life.

The softer side of Torp's nature is shown in his friendship for Dick. Kipling well knew how strong a bond of affection can be forged between men who have shared dangerous experiences together and whose outlook on life is similar. The relationship between Dick and Maisie probably contains an echo of Kipling's own early and frustrated love affairs. Certainly the hero of *The Light that Failed* discovers that at the moment of crisis a man's friendship is more enduring and comforting than a woman's love.

Maisie and Bessie

The two women involved with Dick Heldar are, by comparison with the principal male characters, rather dim and negative, and neither is portrayed with much affection by an author who found it difficult to conceal a latent distrust of the female sex. Maisie, Dick's first sweetheart, is not deliberately cruel but simply fails to understand the nature of his artistic vision or to comprehend the magnitude of his tragedy. The character was directly modelled upon Florence Garrard, a young girl who was another of Aunty Rosa's paying guests at Southsea, with whom the fourteen-year-old Rudyard fell deeply in love. When he returned to India he even proposed marriage to her but time and distance put an end to the affair. When he met her later in London she was completely indifferent and there is no indication that she ever reciprocated his passion. Apparently she was as self-centred, fickle and heartless as her fictional counterpart and doubtless she was scornful of her young admirer's literary pretentions and ambitions. Maisie certainly has no understanding of Dick's aesthetic ideals and all she can say when confronted with his paintings is that they reek of blood and tobacco.

The other female character, Bessie, is a rather more sympathetic figure – a young prostitute who models for Dick. She is in love with his friend Torp and resents Dick's interference, taking a terrible revenge after he goes blind by slashing to shreds the masterpiece for which she has posed. It is the impulsive action of a poor wretched girl for whom art has no meaning and who is incapable of conveying a vestige of human warmth. The original Bessie was a parlour-maid whom Kipling had met in his aunt Georgina's house – a shy, inarticulate working-class girl with whom he could not properly communicate but who obviously made enough of an impression to surface in his memory years later when he wrote his first novel.

The schoolboys

Kipling dedicated *Stalky & Co.* to Cormell Price, headmaster of the United Services College at Westward Ho! which he attended for four years. It was here that he met George Beresford and Lionel Dunsterville, fellow pupils who, like him, were being subjected to the rigours of a public school dedicated to preparing sons of army officers and civil servants for challenging careers in the colonies. Hard work and tough discipline are the traditionally accepted ways of transforming irresponsible, mischievous boys into mature adults and potential empire builders, and the Triple Alliance of Stalky, M'Turk and Beetle indulge in pranks and high jinks, enduring the appropriate punishments, creating a delightful world of boyish fantasy as the surest antidote to the drudgery and misery of school routine.

Stalky is a cunning boy, originator of all the hoaxes and vendettas, wonderfully skilful in avoiding blame and punishment. M'Turk is his willing tool, putting the nefarious plans into motion, and Beetle, a no less eager participant, also contributes satirical diatribes against the masters. The wild escapades could never have happened as

Kipling described them but they make vastly entertaining reading. Doubtless he also exaggerated the violence and the cruelty, although the reality must have been bad enough.

Apart from the fact that the characters in *Stalky & Co.* are modelled on real people it would be a waste of time to look for too many autobiographical parallels in the book. As in all Kipling's works, the characters exist primarily to evoke an atmosphere and recreate a world which was once part of his own experience. *Stalky & Co.* is in a sense a portrait of an entire generation of young men who have been privileged to receive an education that instils them with a sense of responsibility and self-sacrifice, a respect for tradition and a fervent love of their country. Although it appeals to modern readers for its entertainment value and is firmly established as a classic story of boyhood, Kipling did not conceal that he intended it to be a moral tract. Indeed, it is virtually a declaration of his political faith. The boys who get up to such mischief and endure such suffering at school come to recognise that this is all part of growing up, that they are hardening themselves to face the demands of adult life, especially in preparation for the harsh realities of a colonial career. For it is these boys who will be expected to impose Pax Britannica, to defend it honourably and justly,

but, should it prove necessary, by force of arms. The school moulds their character and makes it possible for them to fulfil their missions in life. Stalky becomes a professional soldier, M'Turk an engineer. Beetle, unable to serve his country in such practical ways, decides to write. Of the three, it is he who is destined to make the most lasting contribution to his nation's fortunes.

The soldiers

Kipling's admiration for strict and rigorous discipline in the conduct of daily life is more explicitly spelt out in his stories of military life abroad. He was, above all, a gifted journalist and he brought to all his work the journalist's indispensable capacity for selecting significant points of detail to create an atmosphere or give life to a situation. When he first began writing, some of his strongest impressions were of army life in India. It was natural, therefore, that he should introduce into his tales many of the soldiers and officers he had personally met.

The heroes of the collection of stories called *Soldiers Three* are Mulvaney, Ortheris and Learoyd. In their casual banter, their devotion to one another and their readiness to give of their best in moments of danger, they remind one of Dumas's Three Musketeers. Accustomed

With the teacher away the students come to blows: an
illustration by Raven Hill for Stalky & Co. *(1898).*

to living out in the open, under canvas, they argue, grumble and joke, but they are proudly aware that as a result of the rigid discipline to which they are subjected they are the finest soldiers in the world. It is quite natural for them to criticise their superiors but on no account will they allow outsiders to voice such views. They pine for their homes but know that by the time their service days are over they will be old and useless. Only here in India can they play out their allotted role as servants of their country, and only here will they be recognised as individuals and not run the risk of being humiliated and swamped by people better educated and richer than themselves. In the army they accept differences of rank but not of class. There is a measure of equality here that would be denied them in civilian life.

The colonies and the army were for Kipling proving grounds of manliness and all the human qualities he held most dear – friendship, loyalty, endurance, courage and devotion to duty. For all their rough-and-ready barrack-room language, his three soldiers typify such attitudes. So too do the two drummer-boys, Jakin and Lew, the heroes of *The Drums of Fore and Aft* in another collection of tales, *Wee Willie Winkie*, eventually come to realise that the army is the shaping force in their lives. Jakin, "a stunted child of fourteen",

and Lew, an orphan "furnished with the head of a cherub", are undisciplined scamps whose background is typical of that of many soldiers serving abroad:

". . . They were made up of drafts from an over-populated manufacturing district. The system had put flesh and muscle upon their small bones, but it could not put heart into the sons of those who for generations had done over-much work for over-scanty pay, had sweated in drying-rooms, stooped over looms, coughed among white lead, and shivered on lime barges. The men had found food and rest in the Army, and now they were going to fight "niggers" – people who ran away if you shook a stick at them.

It is not surprising that such lads should not be ready-made heroes and in fact they are by nature timid to the point of cowardice. Only when they find themselves involved in actual fighting does a miracle occur, brought about by circumstances which Kipling describes as follows: The Fore and Fit Band, though protected from direct fire by the rocky knoll under which it had sat down, fled at the first rush. Jakin and Lew would have fled also, but their short legs left them fifty yards in the rear, and by the time the Band had mixed with the Regiment, they were painfully aware that they would have to close in alone and unsupported.

"Get back to that rock,"

Frontispiece for Wee Willie Winkie *(1888).*

94

gasped Jakin. "They won't see us there."

And they returned to the scattered instruments of the Band, their hearts nearly bursting their ribs.

"Here's a nice show for us," said Jakin, throwing himself full length on the ground. "A bloomin' fine show for British Infantry! Oh, the devils! They've gone an' left us alone here! Wot'll we do?"

Lew took possession of a cast-off water-bottle, which naturally was full of canteen rum, and drank till he coughed again.

"Drink," said he shortly. "They'll come back in a minute or two – you see."

This is what happens when Jakin and Lew, trembling with fright but with spirits somewhat bolstered by the rum, crouch behind a rock, cut off from their retreating companions and left to face the Afghans alone. In that moment of shock they discover a spark of heroism that stems from ingrained obedience and sense of duty. The boys walk steadily towards the advancing enemy, Jakin beating the drum and Lew squeaking on the fife to the tune of "The British Grenadiers". This is how Kipling, in a moving passage, describes their death: The two little red dots moved forward in the open parallel to the enemy's front.

The men of the Fore and Fit were gathering thick at the entrance to the plain. The Brigadier on the heights far above was speechless with rage. Still no movement from the enemy. The day stayed to watch the children.

Jakin halted and beat the long roll of the Assembly, while the fife squeaked despairingly.

"Right about face! Hold up, Lew, you're drunk," said Jakin. They wheeled and marched back.

"Here they come!" said Jakin. "Go on Lew".

The Fore and Fit were pouring out of the valley. What officers had said to men in that time of shame and humiliation will never be known; for neither officers or men speak of it now.

"They are coming anew!" shouted a priest among the Afghans. "Do not kill the boys! Take them alive and they shall be of our faith."

But the first volley had been fired, and Lew dropped on his face. Jakin stood for a minute, spun round and collapsed, as the Fore and Fit came forward, the curses of their officers in their ears, and in their hearts the shame of open shame.

Half the men had seen the drummers die, and they made no sign. They did not even shout. They doubled out straight across the plain in open order, and they did not fire.

Even the foreign mercenaries who fight in the ranks of the British army are, by training and example, imbued with similar feelings of loyalty and responsibility. In the same story there is a fine description of the courage exemplified by the crack regiment of Gurkhas:

The Gurkhas were pouring through the left gorge and over the heights at the double to the invitation of the Regimental Quick-step. The black rocks were crowned with dark green spiders as the bugles gave tongue jubilantly.

The Gurkha rear companies tripped and blundered over loose stones. The front files halted for a moment to take stock of the valley and to settle stray bootlaces. Then a happy little sigh of contentment soughed down the ranks, and it was as though the land smiled, for behold there below were the enemy, and it was to meet them that the Gurkhas had doubled so hastily. There was much enemy. There would be amusement. The little men hitched their *kukris* well to hand, and gaped expectantly at their officers as terriers grin ere the stone is cast for them to fetch. The Gurkhas' ground sloped downward to the valley, and they enjoyed a fair view of the proceedings. They sat upon the boulders to watch, for their officers were not going to waste their wind in assisting to repulse a Ghazi rush more than half a mile away. Let the white men look to their own front.

"Hi! yi!" said the Subadar-Major, who was sweating profusely. "Dam' fools yonder, stand close-order! This is no time for close order, it is the time for volleys. Ugh!"

Horrified, amused and indignant, the Gurkhas beheld the retirement of the Fore and Fit with a running chorus of oaths and commentaries.

"They run! The white men run! Colonel Sahib, may we also do a little running?" murmured Runbir Thappa, the senior Jemader.

But the Colonel would have none of it. "Let the beggars be cut up a little," said he wrathfully "Serves 'em right. They'll be prodded into facing round in a minute." They too take pride in being part of an Empire that no foreign power can destroy.

In *Kim* there is an old native soldier who once fought against the British in the Indian Mutiny. He recalls the nineteen battles in which he fought, the forty-six horse skirmishes, the nine wounds he received and, most precious of all, the Order of British India which he wears round his neck. When the Tibetan lama tries to make him understand that fighting is an evil of which he ought not to boast, the confidence of the man that he has acted correctly and justly is not in the slightest way diminished: "And at the last what wilt thou do?" asks the lama. "At the last I shall die," he replies calmly. "And after?" "Let the Gods order it. I have never pestered them with prayers. I do not think They will pester me. Look you, I have noticed in my long life that those who eternally break in upon Those Above with complaints and reports and bellowings and weepings are presently sent for in haste, as our Colonel used to send for slack-jawed down-country men who talked too much. No, I have never wearied the Gods. They will remember this, and give me a quiet place where I can drive my lance in the shade, and wait to welcome my sons: I have no less than three – Rissaldar-majors all – in the regiments."

Mowgli and the jungle

Another of life's proving grounds, in Kipling's view, was the jungle, which inspired some of his most powerfully descriptive passages. This is the school where Mowgli, hero of *The Jungle Book*, grows up. He appears first as a terrified "man-cub" but gradually, by virtue of his intelligence, imposes his will on the animals who have befriended him, until he stands on the threshold of manhood. Mowgli is Kipling's ideal man, totally natural, untouched and unspoiled, capable of learning from his wild environment the laws that must one day govern his adult life. Generations of children have come to enjoy his adventures simply as entertaining fables, but clearly they have a deeper meaning. Thus they can be interpreted as a kind of panorama of primitive existence, before man's appearance on earth. The jungle animals have been there for thousands of years but suddenly they are confronted by a human baby, apt to understand and learn the principles of their own ancient laws. Mowgli is a simple, innocent creature but endowed with the same measure of physical strength as his fellow-animals. Initially his ideas are limited, concentrated on immediate, practical matters associated with sheer survival. He has no dreams, no fantasies. The plans that take shape in his brain, when difficulties arise, are designed merely to surmount impending dangers, without heed of tomorrow. The boy is a stranger to lies, hypocrisy, cruelty and vice. He has no experience of such things for he has had no contact with the corrupt society from which he escaped as a baby. Mowgli is therefore a precursor of man. His intelligence does not yet rise above the level of the inhabitants of the animal kingdom and he remains one of them because he has not discovered such human attributes as pride, deception and wickedness.

Mowgli is an incarnation of the myth of primeval innocence and purity and at the same time voices a sorrowful protest against civilisation. It is as if Kipling wished to negate the 19th-century's proud achievements, notably in science, which were, in his view, dehumanising people and tainting their lives. There are, of course,

Mowgli and the tiger – an illustration by W. H. Drake for The Jungle Book *(1894).*

numerous parallels in European literature, echoing the same urge to return to a primitive way of life as a possible solution to the evils of civilised society. Jean Jacques Rousseau, for example, was convinced that man is contaminated by civilisation, which corrupts and destroys his original propensity for good. Thus his hero, Émile, must be brought up in direct contact with nature in order to equip himself spiritually for the harsh challenges of life. But in Émile's system of education there is always the thought of "tomorrow", the need to prepare for what comes next. There is no such future where Mowgli is concerned, simply a wonderful and happy present among animal friends who can teach him all there is to know about life. When Mowgli eventually returns to the world of men he is incapable of adapting to conventional rules and patterns of behaviour because he has only learned the primitive laws of the jungle.

Daniel Defoe also described the impact of long isolation and the close relationship of man and nature in his famous novel *Robinson Crusoe*. But in the

97

adventures of this shipwrecked sailor on a desert island there is an ever-present awareness of civilised society as a contrasted, corruptive force. Crusoe's first impulse, almost as soon as he awakes on his island, is to get back to his ship and acquire as many articles as may be necessary to ensure his survival. His subsequent struggles against loneliness, wild animals and cannibals represent dramatic attempts not to sink back to the level of primitive life. For Mowgli, on the other hand, the jungle experience is the very point of departure for his human development. When he realises that to remain there is to contravene the laws of nature and to deny his own human dignity, the youth finds the moral strength to abandon his Eden and return to mankind – a conclusion that Kipling provides in order to demonstrate that evasion and renunciation are not solutions to the problem of living. To preserve his spiritual integrity man has to face reality, however cruel that may be. This is the message transmitted by the author of *The Jungle Book*, subtly blending poetry, fantasy, myth and reality in a work of great beauty and imaginative power.

The animals

Around Mowgli move the animals of the jungle – conventional symbols of sheer physical power, wisdom and cunning. Actually the animals are the least successfully realised of all Kipling's characters. They too are conceived as projections of self, derived from personal attitudes and experiences, but in raising them to human level he merely reduces them to puppets so that sometimes they are extremely tiresome and boring. Baloo the bear is the sage, the master, the spokesman – a convenient mouthpiece for the laws that govern the actions of the jungle beasts. Bagheera the panther, who has been imprisoned in a human cage, represents the cunning of those who know life and to whom nothing comes as a surprise. He fears neither the more ferocious animals, such as Shere Khan, the lame tiger, nor man himself, knowing the latter's innate cowardice; yet he sensibly shies away from encounters with both, aware of their superior strength. Kaa the python is the silent force against which nobody can struggle; and Akela the wolf represents the principle of authority in the pack, not unlike that wielded by Queen Victoria over her subjects.

The "law of the jungle" is also typically Victorian in outlook. The phrase has been adopted in common parlance but with a meaning that is almost the very opposite of that which Kipling gave it. It does not, in fact, envisage an inflexible system or hierarchy in which the strongest triumph over the weakest, but a harmonious series of rules and prohibitions that are accepted by all animals in their best interests. They are governed by a kind of parliament which discusses matters of general import in tacit acknowledgment of a civic and penal code. In other words, Kipling's animals are envisaged as humans in another form, all contributing in their various ways to the greatness of the Empire.

In the story called *Her Majesty's Servants* this idea is expressed quite plainly though much less engagingly than in the companion tales. The animals here are stripped of fantasy and simply serve the needs of the troops. They make such an impressive show that an astounded Central Asian chief asks an English officer, "But are the beasts as wise as the men?" To this comes the reply, "They obey, as the men do. Mule, horse, elephant or bullock, he obeys his driver, and the driver his sergeant, and the sergeant his lieutenant, and the lieutenant his captain, and the captain his major, and the major his colonel, and the colonel his brigadier commanding three regiments, and the brigadier his general, who obeys the Viceroy, who is the servant of the Empress."

Thus, it is readily apparent that the military hierarchy also applies to members of the animal kingdom.

Mowgli, Akela and the wolf-cubs (illustration by Drake).

Kim and the lama

The central character of Kipling's hymn to Imperial greatness is the son of an Irish colour-sergeant and a nursemaid. Kipling gave Kim these humble origins deliberately in order to make him more typically one of the people, virtually acknow- ledging the fact that the burden of Empire weighed most heavily on the lower classes, elsewhere embodied in the figure of the ordinary British soldier, Tommy Atkins.

Kim is a boy of exceptional intuition and high intelligence. The talents he may have in- herited by birth from the West- ern world are enriched by the astuteness and wisdom learned from the East. He is therefore the characteristic product of Anglo-Indian civilisation, like the author himself. The vitality and profundity of the Indian soul are reflected in phrases and sentences, rich in humour and meaning, that Kim has picked

99

up in the streets; and it is part of his maturing process to be able to judge people and events in the light of this intuitive Oriental philosophy of life.

For Kipling the figure of Kim is the incarnation of a social and political ideal – the fraternal collaboration of Great Britain and India. The boy is white, and of course remains such, but he is special in that he has come to know and love India from childhood experience. Everything that happens to him in the course of his adventures – even the Great Game of espionage – reinforces the bonds between the two cultures. After all, spying is also a means of serving the vital interests both of Britain and India, and all the characters involved in these events are well aware of this. Mahbub Ali, the rich Afghan horse-trader, does not hesitate to betray his mountain companions, knowing that the welfare of his people is bound up with the prosperity of the Empire and not to be frittered away in sterile rebellion. So he lends himself to the Great Game, at risk to his life, as does Lurgan, the magician-cum-jeweller who introduces Kim to spying. Between them and Creighton, head of British intelligence in India, there is no substantial difference, apart from skin colour. Kim, however, has the advantage over the conventional sahib, who remains separate not only in the racial sense but also in his inability to plumb

the depths of the Indian soul.

Kipling never forgot the happy days of his Indian childhood and Kim is an idealised version of the boy he felt himself to be when he mingled with native children in the markets of Bombay. He begins his story in Lahore, which he only came to know later after his unhappy interlude in England, but the atmosphere he describes is very like that of Bombay where he spent his first impressionable years. Admittedly his background was very different from Kim's, but he too must have experienced "the stealthy prowl through the dark gullies and lanes, . . . the sights and sounds of the women's world on the flat roofs" and seen the "holy men, ash-smeared *fakirs* by their brick shrines under the trees at the riverside".

Kipling's advance towards self-knowledge and maturity was along a very different path than that taken by Kim in the company of the lama, but the Indian experience deeply influenced his somewhat unconventional religious attitudes. His spiritual dilemma – an attempt to reconcile the principles of Christianity with those of the indigenous faiths of India – Buddhism and Hinduism – is to some degree mirrored in the quest of the Tibetan lama. The old priest who has left his monastery to find the River of the Arrow is the most human character – in the sense of goodness and understanding

– that Kipling ever created. His is a special form of goodness, outside daily life, seeming to derive its strength from another world, and he is described in such lyrical and vivid terms that he emerges as much more than an abstract religious symbol. The Buddhism he preaches is certainly unorthodox, strangely intermingled with strains of Hinduism and Christianity, and, in the final analysis, not very convincing. The young Kim listens attentively to him but does not derive from his teachings any valid, practical advice for living. Indeed, on several occasions Kim saves the old man from disaster.

The rather muddled philosophy of the lama, couched though it is in resounding, poetic language, echoes Kipling's own religious confusion. He was stirred and impressed by the faiths of the East but not attracted to any single body of doctrine. The lama arouses feelings of respect and veneration but remains an image of saintliness that the author could admire yet not really explain.

Charles Mears

In *The Finest Story in the World* Kipling took as his theme the supernatural experience of metempsychosis or transmigration of souls, originally an Oriental belief. The hero of the story, Charles Mears, is a bank clerk who lives in an ugly house

Mahbub Ali, the horse-dealer – a terracotta relief by John Lockwood Kipling (1901).

101

Kim and the lama, as depicted by Kipling's father, who was the first illustrator of Kim.

with his elderly mother. He aspires to write a novel. He does not realise that the really valuable thing in his life is his remarkable ability to summon up in dreams the memories of other experiences in remote times, and he throws this away when he falls in love. Once his mind is distracted by passion he loses all contact with his marvellous world of dreams. It is of course a moral story, told with compassion and understanding. The model for the character of Charles Meare was Ambrose Poynter, a cousin of the author and best man at his wedding. The son of the historical painter, Edward Poynter, Ambrose was an architect but had hopes of being a successful poet – an ambition he was not to realise. The idea for the story took shape in the course of discussions between Kipling and Poynter about the nature of the subconscious mind. The latter was firmly convinced that unconscious memories drift to the surface in dreams – a theory developed by the psychologists of the early 20th century – and Kipling gradually conceived the notion of a story in which all these elements could be combined.

Harvey Cheyne

Harvey Cheyne, in *Captains Courageous*, is yet another symbol of the heroic ideal. Son of a rich American, Harvey first appears as a spoiled, arrogant boy with extravagant tastes. A series of improbable accidents introduce him to a completely different world in which he discovers new values and meanings in life. His re-education occurs on board a trawler in the Atlantic as he lives and works alongside a crew of rough, simple fishermen. The inner change is not very convincing, partly because it all happens too quickly and partly because the author is clearly more interested in conveying the general atmosphere of shipboard life and the technicalities of deep-sea fishing than in creating flesh-and-blood characters. Even Dan, the cabinboy, at the opposite end of the social scale, is "good" only by reason of having been reared in what Kipling envisages as a suitable, character-building environment.

Strangely enough, the character best capable of understanding what Kipling meant by the "lesson of life" is Harvey's own father. Towards the end of the book, in a man-to-man lecture, the millionaire recounts the story of his life and delivers some home-spun philosophy on attitudes to business and the virtues of education. The father is speaking:

" 'That's what I *got*. Now I'm coming to what I didn't get. It won't sound much of anything to you, but I don't wish you to be as old as I am before you find out. I can handle men, of course, and I'm no fool along my own lines, but – but – I can't compete with the man who has been *taught*! I've picked up as I went along, and I guess it sticks out all over me. . . . Don't I know it? Don't I know the look on men's faces when they think me a – a "mucker", as they call it out here? I can break them into little pieces – yes – but I can't get back at 'em to hurt 'em where they live. I don't say they're 'way 'way up, but I feel I'm 'way, 'way 'way off, somehow. Now *you've* got your chance. You've got to soak up all the learning that's around, and you'll live with a crowd that are doing the same thing. They'll be doing it for a few thousand dollars a year at most; but remember *you*'ll be doing it for millions. You'll learn law enough to look after your own property when I'm out o' the light, and you'll have to be solid with the best men in the market (they are useful later); and above all, you'll have to stow away the plain, common, sit-down-with-your-chin-on-your-elbows book-learning. Nothing pays like that, Harve, and it's bound to pay more and more each year in our country. . . . You're investing your capital where it'll bring in the best returns; and I guess you won't find our property shrunk any when you're ready to take hold.' "

Kipling, basically a puritan, understood the mentality of a man devoted to the single-

Dan and Harvey Cheyne – an illustration for the first edition of Captains Courageous *(1897).*

minded accumulation of wealth, which he comes to regard as a tangible sign of divine approval. Kipling was not interested in wealth for its own sake but, like so many of his Victorian contemporaries, he tended to equate prosperity with progress and his materialistic out-look is often reflected in his "instructive" works. *Captains Courageous* contains too much moralising in this vein and from the literary viewpoint it cannot bear comparison with the less pretentious Indian stories and the splendidly poetic and im-aginative *Jungle Books.*

The World of Kim

"We Indians shall never cease to be grateful to Kipling for having shown the many faces of our country in all their beauty power and truth."

NIRAD CHAUDHURI

It is from the ancient city of Lahore, now capital of the Pakistani state of Punjab, that Kim and the lama set out on their travels. Although a white boy, Kim "knew the wonderful walled city of Lahore from the Delhi Gate to the outer Fort Ditch", scampering through the winding alleys of the town and mingling with people of all races and creeds, thus earning himself the nickname of "Little Friend of All the World". **Above**: *The Mosque of Wazir Khan, one of most impressive buildings in Lahore (watercolour by William Carpenter).*

Left: Lahore Street Scene *(watercolour by William Carpenter)*. **Right**: Buddha on a Lotus, Meditating — *an alto-relief sculpture from the Lahore Museum, as described minutely by Kipling in Kim: "In open-mouthed wonder the lama turned to this and that, and finally checked in rapt attention before a large alto-relief representing a coronation or apotheosis of the Lord Buddha. The Master was represented seated on a lotus the petals of which were so deeply undercut as to show almost detached. Round Him was an adoring hierarchy of kings, elders, and old-time Buddhas. Below were lotus-covered waters with fishes and water-birds. Two butterfly-winged* dewas *held a wreath over His head; above them another pair supported an umbrella surmounted by the jewelled headdress of the Bodhisat."*

Kipling was well acquainted with the sculptures and friezes of the Lahore Museum, known to the natives as Ajaib-Gher (the Wonder House), because his father was curator. It was such works of art, taken from Buddhist temples and monasteries, which stimulated his deep interest in that religion.

Left: The Tibetan Wheel of Life *(silk painting of 19th century). The theme is a symbolic representation of the Great Wheel which, as explained in* Kim, *"Men say that the Bodhisat Himself drew with grains of rice upon dust, to teach His disciples the cause of things". It is made up of the linked figures of the Hog, Snake and Dove, symbols respectively of Ignorance, Anger and Lust.* **This page**, **above**: *open-work iron pen-case — "the piece of ancient design, Chinese" that the lama gave to the curator of the Lahore Museum as a sign of friendship.* **Below**: *A Group of Ascetics (Sikh watercolour of around 1850). "There were holy men, ash-smeared fakirs by their brick shrine under the trees at the riverside with whom Kim was quite familiar. . . ."*

109

This page, top: Beggars in Front of a Corn-dealer's Shop *(popular Sikh engraving of 1870). In the India of* Kim *beggars often fought one another for a handful of rice or grain. It was in this way that the lama travelled, living on the charity of others. When Kim became his* chela *or disciple he too had to beg for alms.* Left: A Courier from Punjab *(watercolour by Kapur Singh, 1866). During the espionage activities in which Kim was embroiled, frequent use was made of such mail-couriers.* Facing page, above: *Sikh Railway Train (woodcut, 1870). Railway tracks were already snaking across the Punjab and the local population marvelled at the "fire-carriages – work of devils", as the lama called them when he and Kim took the train for Benares.* Right: *the market place at Lucknow (watercolour by William Carpenter). This is the city where Kim, after many adventures, finally found the lama again and set off on the Grand Trunk road.*

Left: View of Benares on the Ganges *(watercolour by William Carpenter, 1856). From Benares, "oldest of all earth's cities awake before the Gods, day and night", the lama and Kim travel in search of the River of the Arrow which brings purification and peace of mind. The boy is indispensable to him, as he says: "Thou was sent for an aid. That aid removed, my Search came to naught. Therefore we will go out again together, and our Search is sure." The new goal of the pilgrims is "a place set about with fruit-trees, where one can walk in meditation". The two companions clamber up steep mountain slopes, through passes deep in snow and long-forgotten villages. "Along their track lay the villages of the hill-folk — mud and earth huts, timbers now and then rudely carved with an axe — clinging like swallows' nests against the steeps, huddled on tiny flats halfway down a three-thousand-foot glissade. . . . and the sallow, greasy, duffle-clad people, with short bare legs and faces almost Esquimaux — would flock out and adore."* **Below**: Himalayan Village *(watercolour by William Simpson, 1860).*

The British in India

Proud of their race and country the officers and civil servants of British India tried to transplant their traditional way of life overseas.

Above: *Captain James Tod riding on the back of an elephant (painted in 1820). A student of Indian history, Tod uncovered the richness of local traditions in a book about the antiquities of Rajasthan, published in 1829–32, which was popular both at home and in India. The men carrying spears are sepoys, ordinary Indian soldiers trained on European lines and commanded by British officers. In 1856, discontented for a variety of reasons, the sepoys rose in mutiny against the British, sparking off a bloody war which culminated in an Indian defeat in the winter of 1857–8.*

Below: *in March 1846, after their victory in the Punjab, the British resident Henry Lawrence, the commander Lord Gough and governor Sir Henry Hardinge sign a peace treaty with the defeated Sikh leaders at Lahore (contemporary painting). Once a province of the Mogul Empire, then an independent Sikh state, the Punjab had supported the British in their fight against the Marathas. After the death of their ruler Ranjit Singh in 1839 the Sikhs had changed their policy and invaded British-held territory. The Treaty of Lahore only marked a brief halt in the conflict; a new rebellion broke out in March 1849 and the Punjab was annexed to the Empire.* **Right**: *two episodes in the Indian Mutiny.* **Above**: The Attack on Delhi *(watercolour of 1857)*, **Below**: British Troops on the March *(contemporary lithograph).*

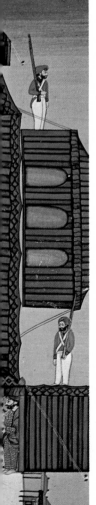

Above, left: Military Parade in Bombay *(watercolour by O. Norie, 1864).* **Above, right**: Prisoners Before a Magistrate, *a popular woodcut dating from 1870, belonging to John Kipling's collection of Indian prints. In the courts set up by the British, justice was dispensed by British officials according to their own country's procedures and laws. This led many middle-class Indians to study law, with the result that lawyers soon formed the largest and most influential professional group in the land.* **Right**: *a British commander reads out the act of proclamation in the Punjab, declaring Queen Victoria Empress of India (watercolour by R. Simkin, 1887).*

The families of British civil servants and army officers living in India did their best to maintain their traditional life style abroad, playing cricket and polo, arranging garden parties, reading the English classics – customs that were imitated by the Indian middle classes. **Above, left**: *an English lady being carried in a litter in the Simla neighbourhood (19th-century watercolour).* **Below, left**: *dinner in the house of a British officer (watercolour, 1860).* **Below**: *a garden party at Onnedale in the Himalayas (lithograph by A. E. Scott, 1845).*

The tiger hunt, favourite 'sport' of the maharajahs and Indian nobility, and a passion shared by the British colonialists. **Above**: *a dramatic hunting scene depicted by an anonymous artist from Patiala at the end of the nineteenth century.*

Kipling and the Critics

"Time, and severe impartial standards, winnowing his work, will winnow much of it away; but they will certainly leave something that is unique."

EDWARD SHANKS

Not quite a genius

Few writers of modern times have been subjected to such a barrage of conflicting criticism as Rudyard Kipling. Time and place have imposed judgments so contradictory that it is sometimes hard to realise they apply to the same writer. For certain critics Kipling remains the towering literary genius of the Victorian age; for others he is the sullied symbol of the British Empire in decline. Those who have found his more jingoistic vein of poetry an embarrassment have conveniently dismissed his vast poetical output and concentrated their attention wholly on the prose, only to find themselves running into more trouble in their attempts to sift the good from the bad. Most critics have encountered the basic difficulty of separating Kipling the political man from Kipling the artist, and the more astute commentators have finally recognised that this is impossible for his art was inextricably linked with his life. In recent years there has been a reappraisal and partial rehabilitation of a writer whom previous generations had undervalued or accepted on sufferance. But even modern critics will not unequivocally describe him as a genius.

The critical fortunes of Kipling, the prophet of imperialism, swung from one extreme to another even during his lifetime, ranging from almost hysterical acclaim during the last years of the 19th century to studied indifference, even hostility, from readers and critics alike, in the early part of the present century and indeed up to his death in 1936. Even the award of the Nobel Prize for Literature did little to bolster his fading reputation. In 1919 E. T. Raymond announced glibly: "Mr Rudyard Kipling is not perhaps a spent force. But it seems safe to say that he will never again be more than a minor one." For his part, Kipling tended to ignore his critics, not much caring whether they praised or denounced him. He formed close friendships with influential literary figures such as Henry James and Robert Louis Stevenson, and he was generous in his eulogies of colleagues, but he never curried favour or solicited their approval.

Kipling's first books were reviewed fairly widely by English newspapers in India, but it would have needed extraordinary perception on the part of critics in Bombay and Lahore to realise that this young colleague of theirs possessed the seeds of genius or to predict that he might one day become a writer of international repute. At the time he was recognised as a provincial journalist of undoubted talent, but little more. The themes of his early stories found a ready response with the Anglo-Indian reading public because they were part of common experience but they did not shock, surprise or arouse controversy. In any case the educated members of this community, rubbing shoulders with the young author in clubs, offices and drawing rooms, were quite familiar with his social and moral attitudes and his political beliefs which, by and large, echoed their own. He was liked and admired, especially for his unassuming and modest manner and his readiness to seek the advice of others. Few in India regarded him as a provocative or contentious figure.

The consequence was that for some years Kipling's literary efforts, as distinct from his newspaper articles, were considered competent exercises, entertaining but hardly meriting serious discussion. The *Departmental Ditties*, published in 1886, were described by the reviewer of the *Times of India* as "a very pleasant companion for a lonely half-hour, or to while away the tedium of a railway journey." The *Indian Daily News* proclaimed the verses "bright and clever, with occa-

121

sional touches which indicate that the author may some day reach to higher flights. . . ." These are the kind of comments of a schoolmaster wearily preparing a pupil's progress report.

Kipling's first job was on the Lahore *Civil and Military Gazette*, and it was this paper's editor, E. Kay Robinson, who first realised that his assistant had the makings of an exceptional journalist. Robinson recognised that the young man's literary ambitions were genuine and sincere, stemming not from a casual desire to make a living but from a deep-rooted, spontaneous urge for self-expression. What impressed him were Kipling's attention to minute detail, his ability to pen vivid descriptive sketches, his intuitive capacity for portraiture and his remarkable skill in reproducing natural dialogue. One flaw in his makeup was that he had no idea how to cover sports events which, as Kipling later admitted, simply did not interest him. In due course Robinson wrote to an ex-colleague about the way in which he helped launch Kipling on his career: "Having to my great delight 'discovered' Kipling (though his name was already a household word throughout India) in 1886, I thought that the literary world at home should share my pleasure. He

was just then publishing his first little book in India; but the *Departmental Ditties* were good enough, as I thought at the time, and as afterwards turned out, to give him a place among English writers of the day. So I obtained eight copies, and distributed them, with recommendatory letters, among editors of English journals. . . . So far as I could ascertain, not a single one of those papers condescended to say a word about the unpretentious little volume."

Robinson was mistaken, for one copy of the book found its way onto the desk of Andrew Lang, a poet, essayist and critic who then wrote a monthly column for *Longman's Magazine*. Lang read the collection of verse, liked it and noted with satisfaction that the author had apparently not provided his name, presumably out of modesty. Actually the facsimile of Kipling's signature appeared on the front cover. Lang wrote about the poems in his monthly column for *Longman's Magazine* in October 1886. It was the first review of Kipling's work in England. It was lukewarm, describing the verses as "quaint and amusing" and remarking, "Would that all poems were as brief." Three years later, reviewing "Mr Kipling's Stories", Lang acknowledged that "on

the whole, the two little volumes, with Mr Kipling's *Departmental Ditties*, give the impression that there is a new and enjoyable talent at work in Anglo-Indian literature." In another unsigned review of *Plain Tales from the Hills*, after pointing out certain shortcomings, Lang concluded that "it is natural to expect much from a talent so fresh, facile, and spontaneous, working in a field of such unusual experiences."

"Eureka! A genius has come to light!"

Kipling's first notable success in England was his *Soldiers Three*, published in March 1889 and reviewed anonymously in the *Spectator* in that month. The article ended: "The perusal of these stories cannot fail to inspire the reader with the desire to make further acquaintance with the other writings of the author. They are brimfull of humanity and a drollery that never degenerates into burlesque. In many places a note of genuine pathos is heard. Mr Kipling is so gifted and versatile, that one would gladly see him at work on a larger canvas. But to be so brilliant a teller of short stories is in itself no small distinction." Later Kipling received the stamp of approval from the influential Andrew Lang who is said to have exclaimed, after reading *Soldiers Three*: "Eureka! A genius has come to light!"

With the weight of Lang's authority behind him, Kipling's entry into the world of letters was automatic and his subsequent rise to fame meteoric. J. M. Barrie, reviewing *The Light that Failed*, was not over-keen but admitted there were "latent capabilities . . . which may develop". Oscar Wilde called him "a genius who drops his aspirates" and Edmund Gosse explained "why the sense of these shortcomings is altogether buried for me in delighted sympathy and breathless curiosity". In 1893 Sir Arthur Quiller-Couch, better known as "Q", who had edited *The Oxford Book of English Verse* compared Kipling's poetry with W. E. Henley's and commented that while Kipling worked from life, Henley drew on his literary learning: "Mr Kipling finds the East enchanting, for instance, by right of having been born there; Mr Henley by right of having made acquaintance with it in the pages of the *Arabian Nights Entertainment* . . ." Other literary figures to recognise the merits of Kipling's works around the turn of the century included G. K. Chesterton, Alfred Noyes and Sir Arthur Conan Doyle.

Spurred on by the critics, the English reading public added its accolades; and although certain reviewers sounded more sour notes, his renown and fortune were guaranteed. Yet his subsequent fall from favour was almost as sudden as his earlier climb to fame. Initial public enthusiasm stemmed largely from the fact that in the early books he looked back nostalgically to the India of his childhood, reflecting a nation's pride in its Imperial achievement. This acclaim encouraged him to turn his natural capacity for hard work away from literature towards a more active participation in the country's political life. His articles and poetry were ever more closely linked to the events of the day, reflecting the opinions and supporting the decisions of the ruling Conservative government. Soon he came to be regarded virtually as the official government apologist, a label that was inevitably detrimental to his artistic endeavours. Although his books continued to be read and enjoyed all over the world, the critics tended to ignore him. For almost two decades, from the opening of the century and right through the First World War, newspapers at home and abroad almost stopped printing authoritative reviews of his books, although his publishers, encouraged by the steady sales figures, kept his novels and short stories on the market.

The scant attention paid to his works by 20th-century critics and scholars gradually cast doubt in the mind of the public as to the validity of his political statements and opinions. Little by little Kipling acquired a reputation for being an outdated bird of ill-omen, especially for his gloomy predictions concerning the future of an Empire that had flourished throughout the Victorian age and carried the message of civilisation to all parts of the world. The pessimistic warnings which he issued in the 1930s prior to the Second World War were of no avail. Nobody who counted would pay any heed to this latter-day Cassandra.

The first serious attempt at reappraisal came in 1919 when the distinguished poet and critic T. S. Eliot wrote a review in the *Atheneum* entitled "Kipling Redivivus", opening with the words: "Mr Kipling is a laureate without laurels. He is a neglected celebrity." Eliot too recognised Kipling's faults and dubbed him "nearly a great writer", but his interest spurred other critics in the 1920s and towards the end of Kipling's life to look at his works with a fresh, objective eye. Bonamy Dobrée, writing in 1927, suggested that "it will only be possible to give him his rightful place when the political heats of his day have become coldly historical. But to us, the successive generation, he has a value that may well be permanent. . . ." In an obituary notice published in the *Times Literary Supplement*, the anonymous contributor voiced doubts as to the merits of Kipling's poetry but described him as "one of the most virile and skilful of English masters of the short story . . . among the greatest of the pioneers." The notice concluded that the "juries of the future . . . must add to their verdict a rider that this was a great man as well as a great writer; and honourable and fearless and good."

In the light of post-war events Kipling suffered another reversal of fortunes, especially in an India exposed to the traumatic experiences of partition and independence. When he first won acclaim in London, the Anglo-Indian community basked in his reflected glory. The legends and stories of the now-successful writer, who had sprung from their midst, were a welcome relief from the stresses and strains of daily life, a form of escapism in an alien environment, even from the grim reality of death itself which, in a country so ravaged by disasters and epidemics, was an everyday occurrence. Between the wars his reputation declined, as it did elsewhere, and when the nation, under the spiritual and political guidance of Mahatma Gandhi and his colleagues, won independence, Kipling was abruptly dropped from favour. By that time his works were contemptuously dismissed by critics since they were held to contain propaganda messages on behalf of political ideas and institutions now judged outmoded and irrelevant. Indian writers proud of their country's independence vigorously denounced the author who symbolised decades of colonial oppression and injustice. Yet as the turbulent years passed and India settled uneasily into her new world role, Kipling enjoyed a slow revival. The critic Nirad C. Chaudhuri analysed the changing attitudes of his countrymen towards Kipling, with particular reference to *Kim* which he described as "not only the finest novel in the English language with an Indian theme, but also one of the greatest of English novels in spite of the theme . . . great by any standards that ever obtained in any age of English literature." Chaudhuri's essay, first published in the magazine *Encounter* in April 1957, was later included in a compendium of Kipling's life and works,* which appeared in 1972, to which nineteen other distinguished writers contributed.

"Infant monster"

Kipling's appearance on the literary scene during the last years of the 19th century had something of the impact of a tornado ripping through a stretch of peaceful countryside. Oscar Wilde had coined the term "art for art's sake" and to those cultured minds who regarded perfection of form as being the key essential to a masterpiece Kipling's first published works – racy and vulgar – seemed profoundly shocking. His rough manner and realistic dialogue were admirably suited to the short story, thus far the prerogative of French writers. In English literature the only serious form of prose fiction was the novel and it was not until Kipling brought out his first novel, *The Light that Failed*, that critics began paying much

Rudyard Kipling, the Man, his Work and his World (Weidenfeld and Nicolson).

attention to the new "star" on the literary horizon. But his real importance was in being the creator of the short story form in England and this was the secret of his popularity and success with all classes of readership.

Kipling's journalistic experience in India made a lasting impression on his style – forthright, concise and often brutally realistic. His appeal was directly to the senses and emotions, inviting his readers to participate in the events being described – evoking for them the sights, the sounds, the smells of a mysterious and wonderful world. Such a blatantly direct approach was bound to offend and disgust those who professed to be the arbiters of good taste, the high priests of "culture"; and even those who dared to suggest that there might be a genius in the making sometimes felt it necessary to apologise for being seen in such low company.

Henry James, as is evident from his letters had a curious love-hate relationship towards Kipling. Writing to Stevenson in January 1891, James summed up his first impressions as follows: "The only news in literature here – such is the virtuous vacancy of our consciousness – continues to be the infant monster of a Kipling." A year later, in a letter to his brother William, he was far less flippant and much warmer in his praise: "Kipling strikes me personally," he wrote, "as the most complete man of genius (as distinct from fine intelligence) that I have ever known." Four years later, discussing *The Seven Seas*, he confessed to Jonathan Sturges: "I am laid low by the absolutely uncanny talent – the prodigious special faculty of it. It's all *violent*, without a dream of nuance or a hint of 'distinction'; all prose trumpets and castanets and such – with never a touch of the fiddle-string or a note of the nightingale. But it's magnificent and masterly in its way, and full of the most insidious art. He's a rum 'un – and one of the very few first *talents* of the time."

Yet within a year James's enthusiasm had for some reason begun to wane. Why? Kipling was revealing himself as a writer of sudden fits and starts who appeared not to care a hoot about the fashionable world of letters. He did not choose to retire into an intellectual ivory tower but to pour out his feelings spontaneously and openly, finding his inspiration in the visible world of people, places and events. The Indian stories, inextricably linked to the soil of the land where he had spent his carefree childhood, were written in a lively forceful manner with little conscious artistry; the poems too, reflecting his views on politics and Britain's Imperial role, were drawn from the hurly-burly of everyday life, their rough language and rollicking rhythms defying all the conventional rules of approved versification. Literary purists such as Henry James could hardly be expected to condone such vulgarity and by the end of 1897 he was admitting to being sadly disappointed: "In his earliest time," he wrote to Grace Norton, "I thought he perhaps contained the seeds of an English Balzac; but I have given that up in proportion as he has come down steadily from the simple in subject to the more simple – from the Anglo-Indians to the natives, from the natives to the Tommies, from the Tommies to the quadrupeds, from the quadrupeds to the fish, and from the fish to the engines and screws."

Two years later James expressed his sense of disillusionment in even stronger language to Charles Eliot Norton: "I am afraid you will think me a very disgusted person if I show my reserves again, over *his* recent incarnations. I can't swallow his loud, brazen patriotic verse – an exploitation of the patriotic idea. . . . Two or three times a century – yes; but not every month."

125

The bright lantern

A writer who showed far more generosity and perception in analysing the early works of Kipling was the Scottish playwright James Barrie, best known as the creator of that perennial childhood favourite, *Peter Pan*. Barrie was a man of broad interests and at one time seemed likely to rival Kipling as a novelist; but he came to be remembered for a series of highly entertaining plays, introducing a refreshingly lightweight vein of dream and fantasy to the London stage, currently dominated by the heavier guns of Shaw and Ibsen.

Barrie, of course, had himself dabbled in the short story form (*Peter Pan* being derived from a series of tales based on childhood memories) and therefore it is not surprising that a bond of understanding was immediately established.

As early as 1891, the year in which he published his bestselling novel *The Little Minister*, Barrie wrote a long article in the *Contemporary Review*, analysing Kipling's early books in some detail: "Now that the Eurekas over his discovery are ended," he observed, "we have no reason to blush for them. . . . Here is a literary 'sensation' lifted on high because he is worth looking at. Doubtless the circumstances were favourable. Most writers begin with one book, but he came from India with half a dozen ready, and fired them at the town simultaneously. A six-shooter attracts more attention than a single barrel."

Barrie's praise of Kipling was based on more than friendship and he went on to discuss the short stories and the first novel fairly and objectively: "From the first only risky subjects seem to have attracted Mr Kipling. He began by dancing on ground that most novelists look long at before they adventure a foot. His game was leapfrog over all the passions. One felt that he must have been born *blasé*, that in his hurry to be a man he had jumped boyhood. . . ." That was a searching comment, indeed, for Kipling had achieved emotional maturity very young. When he went to work for his first newspaper in Lahore at the age of sixteen his face, with sideburns and rimless spectacles, certainly belied his years. Perhaps because of this hurry, continued Barrie, ". . . his boy and girl of *The Light that Failed* are a man and woman playing in vain at being children." And he pinpointed the distinctive feature of Kipling's style almost better than any other critic in suggesting: "The task he set himself was to peer into humanity with a very bright lantern, of which he holds the patent, and when he encountered virtue he passed it by respectfully as not what he was looking for. It is a jewel, no doubt, but one that will not gleam sufficiently in the light of that lantern. In short, he was in search of the devil (his only hero so far) that is in all of us, and he found him and brought him forth for inspection, exhibiting him from many points of view in a series of lightning flashes. Lightning, however, dazzles as well as reveals, and after recovering their breath, people began to wonder whether Mr Kipling's favourite figure would look like this in daylight. He has been in no hurry to answer them, for it is in these flashes that the magic lies; they are his style."

For the creator of Peter Pan Kipling's true stature lay in his ability to illuminate his characters with these sudden and unexpected bursts of light, and he continued: "Some admit his humour, his pathos, his character-drawing, his wonderful way of flashing a picture before our eyes till it is as vivid as a landscape seen in lightning – in short, his dramatic power – and yet add with a sigh, 'What a pity he has no style!' This surely is saying in one breath that he is and he isn't. These qualities they have allowed him are his style."

From the moment Kipling took London by storm the strongest criticism levelled against him was that he lacked taste, that his rough-and-ready style of writing flew in the face of all accepted literary canons. Barrie dismissed this as foolish and went on to compare Kipling's style with that of the much-admired Stevenson: "He is to Stevenson as phonetic spelling is to pure English. He is not a Christian but a Kristyān. His words are often wrong, but he groups them so that they convey the idea he is in pursuit of. We see at once that his pathos is potatoes. It is not legitimate, but it produces the desired effects. There are sentences without verbs. He wants perpetually to take his readers by surprise, and has them, as it were, at the end of a string, which he is constantly jerking. With such a jerk he is usually off from one paragraph to the next. He writes Finis with it. His style is the perfection of what is called journalese. . . ."

One of Kipling's obvious failings as a writer was his inability to understand fully the subtle psychology of women. None of the heroines of his books are portrayed with sufficient understanding or penetration to make them unforgettable. Some

are more appealing, more alive, than others, but they are usually blurred in outline, as if only dimly seen by the author himself. This applies to such characters as Mowgli's mother, the rich Hindu lady in *Kim* and to Maisie in *The Light that Failed*. Barrie suspected this shortcoming and in the same article commented: "The 'duel between the sexes' . . . is Mr Kipling's theme (which increases his chances of immortality), and there is a woman in most of his stories. Yet who remembers her? The three soldiers' tales are often about women, and these wonderful soldiers you could not forget if you would, but the women are as if they had never been. . . . In *The Light that Failed*, Maisie, the heroine, is utterly uninteresting, which is the one thing a heroine may not be. We never know her, and this is not because she is an intricate study. She is merely offered as a nice girl, with an ambition to have her person and paintbrush described in the *Star's* fashionable column. But she is colourless, a nonentity. On the other hand, she has a friend called 'the red-haired girl', whom we do care for, but probably only because we see her in three brief flashes. If she came into the light of day she might prove as dull as Maisie."

The real India

Critics during Kipling's lifetime were sharply divided in their attitudes towards Kipling's picture of India under British rule, and even today the doubts linger on. He has been reproved for offering the public a view of a world that bore little if any resemblance to reality, sometimes a poetic and legendary world but surely one far removed from actual events and situations. This view again reflects the ambivalence of critics who hanker to admire yet feel obliged to detract. Barrie had no patience with those who condemned Kipling for failing to conform or flatter, but acknowledged some justice in the criticism. "Some have taken Mr Kipling's aim to be the representation of India as it is, and have refused to believe that Indian life – especially Anglo-Indian life – is as ugly as he paints it. Their premiss granted, few would object to their conclusion except such as judge England by the froth of society or by its dregs. But Mr Kipling warns us against this assumption. In the preface to one of his books . . . he 'assures the ill-informed that India is not entirely inhabited by men and women playing tennis with the Seventh Commandment. . . . The drawback of collecting dirt in one corner is that it gives a false notion of the filth of the room.' The admission of his aim herein contained contracts his ambition into a comparatively little thing, but it should silence much of the hostile criticism. That he is entitled as an artist to dwell chiefly on the dirty corner of the room will surely be admitted . . . (but) we want to see the whole room lighted up so that we may judge the dirty corner by comparison. No doubt it is this want of perspective that has made many uneasy about Mr Kipling's work.''

Barrie suspected, even as early as 1891, that Kipling's real forte was the short story and that, furthermore, his heart would ever remain in India: ''We have no right to demand long novels from him, we should be content to revel in his sketches, but if, as we have been led to believe, his intentions run in that direction, we know enough of him to be convinced that he should lay his scene in India. The cry for an English novel has been curiously unreasonable. The example our great novelists have set him is not to write of England, but of what he knows best. If by an accident it has usually been England with them, it is India by accident with him.''

The judgments of Andrew Lang were expressed somewhat more poetically than those of Barrie but at times rather pompously. He too had great admiration for Kipling yet was not blind to his shortcomings. ''The wind bloweth where it listeth,'' was how he began a critical essay in January 1891. ''But the wind of literary inspiration has rarely shaken the bungalows of India. . . . That old haunt of history, the wealth of character brought out in that confusion of races, of religions, and the old and the new, has been wealth untouched, a treasure-house sealed: those pagoda trees have never been shaken. At last there comes an Englishman with eyes, with a pen extraordinarily deft, an observation marvellously rapid and keen; and, by good luck, this Englishman has no official duties: he is neither a soldier, nor a judge; he is merely a man of letters. He has leisure to look around him, he has the power of making us see what he sees; and, when we have lost India, when some new power is ruling where we ruled, when our empire has followed that of the Moguls, future generations will learn from Mr Kipling's works what India was under English sway.''

This was a penetrating judgement indeed and interesting,

too, in its recognition that British rule in India would not necessarily last for ever, as the majority of Lang's countrymen fondly believed. Now that the colonial days are over, Lang's predictions have proved valid. No number of scholarly theses and historical surveys have contributed as much to Western understanding of India as have Kipling's short stories and his novel *Kim*.

Lang continued: ''Mr Kipling's work, like all good work, is both real and romantic. It is real because he sees and feels very swiftly and keenly; it is romantic, for the attraction and possibility of adventure, and because he is young. . . . In brief, Mr Kipling has conquered worlds, of which, as it were, we knew not the existence.'' Then, in fairness, Lang pointed out: ''His faults are so conspicuous, so much on the surface, that they hardly need to be named. They are curiously visible to some readers who are blind to his merits.''

Another admirer of Kipling was Oscar Wilde, author of so many witty plays, poems, essays and casual epigrams, the acknowledged leader of London's social and cultural life until he scandalised it and paid the penalty. No two writers could have been more different yet Wilde relished Kipling's vigorous realism and recognised that he possessed the touch of genius. In an article for the *Nineteenth Century*, written in 1890, Wilde noted: "He who would stir us now by fiction must either give us an entirely new background or reveal to us the soul of man in its innermost workings. The first is for the moment being done for us by Mr Rudyard Kipling. As one turns over the pages of his *Plain Tales from the Hills*, one feels as if one were seated under a palm-tree reading life by superb flashes of vulgarity. The jaded, second-rate Anglo-Indians are in exquisite incongruity with their surroundings. The mere lack of style in the story-teller gives an odd journalistic realism to what he tells us. From the point of view of literature Mr Kipling is a genius who drops his aspirates. From the point of view of life, he is a reporter who knows vulgarity better than anyone has ever known it."

Dishonoured prophet

Today Kipling's poetry is, though no longer dismissed as valueless, generally considered to be of far less importance than the bulk of his prose. When his Indian verses first appeared in England the majority of critics

and readers, brought up on the lyrical works of Wordsworth, Shelley, Keats and Tennyson, were shocked by their vulgarity and unconventionality, hardly deigning to mention them in the same breath as those of the most fashionable poets of the age. Nevertheless even then there were a few critics who were prepared to assess Kipling's poetry on its merits, the first being Charles Eliot Norton, Professor of the History of Art at Harvard University and best known as an editor of Carlyle's letters and as a translator of Dante's *Divine Comedy*. In an article in the *Atlantic Monthly* for January 1897 Norton wrote: "As we look back over the poetry of the century, two main inspiring motives, exhibiting a natural evolution of poetic doctrine and influence, are clearly distinguishable. The one, of which Wordsworth is the representative, proceeded direct from external nature in her relations to man; while the other, with many representatives from Keats to Tennyson, Arnold, Clough and Browning, was derived from human nature, from man himself in his various relations to the universe and to his kind. . . . The poetry inspired by these motives was the adequate expression of the ideals of the age – of its shifting creeds, its doubts, its moral

perplexities, its persistent introspection. The mood lasted for full fifty years. . . . But meanwhile the process of mental and spiritual evolution was going on. The mood was gradually changing; the poets themselves, by uttering it, were exhibiting its limitations. . . . A new generation . . . found the poetic motives of the earlier part of the century insufficient; neither external nature nor human nature in any select aspect was what it cared most about. It had taken to heart the instructions of the poets; it aimed 'to see life steadily and see it *whole*'. . . . It took the whole world for its realm and was moved to depict it in its actual aspect and what was called its reality. . . . The new spirit showed itself at first in prose fiction. It was weak and often misdirected. It waited for its poet. For realism – the aim to see the world and depict it as it is – required . . . the highest exercise of the poetic imagination. . . . To see a thing truly, a man must, as Blake says, look *through*, not *with* the eye. The common reporter sees *with* the eye, and, meaning to tell the truth, tells a falsehood. But the imagination has insight, and what it sees is reality.

"It is now some six or seven years since *Plain Tales from the Hills* gave proof that a man who

129

saw through his eyes was studying life in India and was able to tell us what he saw. And those who read the scraps of verse prefixed to many of his stories, if they knew what poetry was, learned that their writer was at least potentially a poet, not by virtue of fantasy alone, but by his mastery of lyrical versification. The rhythm of these fragments had swing and ease and variety. . . . *The Seven Seas* contains a notable addition to the small treasury of enduring English verse, an addition sufficient to establish Mr Kipling's right to take place in the honourable body of those English poets who have done England service in strengthening the foundations of her influence and her fame. The dominant tone of his verse is indeed the patriotic; and it is the tone of the new patriotism, that of imperial England, which holds as one all parts of her widestretched empire, and binds them close in the indissoluble bond of common motherhood, and with the ties of common convictions, principles, and aims, derived from the teachings and traditions of the motherland, and expressed in the best verses of her poets. . . . From the reek of the barrackroom we come out with delight to the open air and to the fresh breezes of the sea. For the sea has touched Mr Kipling's imagination with its magic and its mystery, and never are his sympathies keener than with the men who go down upon it, and with the vast relations of human life to the waters that encircle the earth. Here too is manifest his love of England, the mistress of the sea."

Norton openly took up cudgels against Henry James who objected so strongly to Kipling's fervent flag-waving and obsession with engines and screws, continuing: "And so vivid are his appreciations of the poetic significance of even the most modern and practical of the conditions and aspects of sea life that in 'McAndrew's Hymn', a poem of surpassing excellence alike in conception and execution, Mr Kipling has sung the song of the marine steam-engine and all its machinery, from furnace-bars to screw, in such wise as to convert their clanging beats and throbs into a sublime symphony in accord with the singing of the morning stars."

The songs and stories in which soldiers featured as heroes were equally effective expressions of Kipling's patriotic faith. *The Barrack-Room Ballads* were virtually hymns of praise to the British troops in colonial India. They immediately captured the imagination of readers at home and some of them became even more popular when set to music. Yet some critics were noticeably less impressed by these patriotic effusions than the mass of the reading public. One of the first dissenting voices was that of Edmund Gosse, best known for his autobiography *Father and Son* but also respected as a critic and for having introduced to England a number of French and Scandinavian masterpieces. In an article in the *Century Magazine*, October 1891, Gosse frankly admitted to having mixed feelings about the author of *Soldiers Three*. "I cannot pretend," he wrote, "to be indifferent to the charm of what Mr Kipling writes. From the first moment of my acquaintance with it it has held me fast. It excites, disturbs, and attracts me; I cannot throw off its disquieting influence. I admit all that is to be said in its disfavour. I force myself to see that its occasional cynicism is irritating and strikes a false note. I acknowledge the broken and jagged style, the noisy newspaper bustle of the little peremptory sentences, the cheap irony of the satires on society. . . . I shall try to explain why the sense of these shortcomings is altogether buried for me in delighted sympathy and breathless curiosity. Mr Kipling does not provoke a critical suspension of judgment. He is vehement, and sweeps us away with him; he plays upon a strange and seductive pipe, and we follow him like children."

Gosse confessed to admiration, too, for Kipling's portrayal of the British soldier: "We have hitherto had in English literature no portraits of private soldiers like these. . . . Other studies of this kind in fiction have either been slight and unsubstantial . . . or else odious in their sentimental unreality. . . . The absence of sentimentality in Mr Kipling's version of the soldier's life in India is one of its great merits. . . . We see the ignorant and raw English youth transplanted, at the very moment when his instincts begin to develop, into a country where he is divided from everything which can remind him of home. . . . How he behaves himself under these new circumstances, what code of laws still binds his conscience, what are his relaxations, and what his observations, these are the questions which we ask and which Mr Kipling essays for the first time to answer."

Gosse was more scathing about Kipling's earliest published verse: "Mr Kipling's début was made in a volume of verse, called *Departmental Ditties.* . . . This collection of comi-

cal and satirical pieces representative of Indian official life has, however, very slight literary value. The verses in it are mostly imitations of popular English and American bards, with but here and there a trace of the true accent of the author. . . . No claim for the title of poet could be founded on literary baggage so slight as *Departmental Ditties.*" He did, nevertheless, have a kind word for the *Barrack-Room Ballads* which he declared "unique in their kind, and of which scarcely one but is of definite and permanent value."

The first really vicious critical attacks on Kipling, not so much for literary reasons as for his alleged warmongering and conservatism, came towards the end of the century. Among those who helped to topple Kipling from his pedestal of fame was a little known poet, novelist and playwright named Robert Buchanan who had previously waged bitter war against the Pre-Raphaelite artists and, in 1871, on Dante Gabriel Rossetti in particular. Now, in December 1899, two months after the outbreak of the South African war, he brought his guns to bear on the revered prophet of Empire in a *Contemporary Review* article provocatively entitled "The Voice of the Hooligan". It had little

relevance to Kipling's literary output but it was devastatingly influential in reversing the trend of public opinion, heralding a reaction that caused the writer's reputation to plummet steadily downward over the next twenty years. However, in recent years there has been a new interest in his work.

Speaking of the "great backwave in the direction of absolute barbarism" that he had detected in the last few decades, Buchanan continued: "The first noticeable change came, perhaps, with the criminal crusade of the Crimean war; and from that hour to this . . . the enthusiasm of humanity among the masses has gradually, but surely, died away. . . . The world at large, repudiating the enthusiasm of humanity altogether, and exchanging it for the worship of physical force and commercial success in any and every form, has turned rapturously towards activities which need no sanction whatever, or which, at any rate, can be easily sanctified by the wanton will of the majority. Men no longer, in the great civic centres at least, ask themselves whether a particular course of conduct is right or wrong, but whether it is expedient, profitable, and certain of clamorous approval. . . . There is a universal scramble

131

for plunder, for excitement, for amusement, for speculation, and, above it all, the flag of a Hooligan Imperialism is raised, with the proclamation that it is the sole mission of Anglo-Saxon England ... to expand and extend its boundaries indefinitely, and, again in the name of the Christianity it has practically abandoned, to conquer and inherit the earth."

Buchanan then turned to "our popular literature ... long past praying for", and began his onslaught on Kipling who "in his single figure adumbrates, I think, all that is most deplorable, all that is most retrograde and savage, in the restless and uninstructed Hooliganism of the time." He granted that Kipling's Anglo-Indian writings had initially struck an original note and deserved popularity, few writers having thus far dealt with "the ignobler details of military and civilian life, with the gossip of the mess-room and the scandal of the government departments." Buchanan then went on: "Mr Kipling's little Kodak-glimpses, therefore, seemed unusually fresh and new; nor would it be just to deny them the merits of great liveliness, intimate personal knowledge, and a certain unmistakable, though obviously cockney, humour. . . . At any rate, whatever their

merits were – and I hold their merits to be indisputable – they became rapidly popular, especially with the newspaper press, which hailed the writer as a new and quite amazing force in literature. So far as the lazy public was concerned, they had the one delightful merit of extreme brevity. . . . Two factors contributed to their vogue; first, the utter apathy of general readers ... and, second, the rapid growth in every direction of the military or militant spirit ... in a word, of Greater Englandism, or Imperialism."

As the self-appointed "approved and authoritative poet of the British Empire" Kipling published the Barrack-Room Ballads, to which Buchanan now took strong exception, condemning them for being a picture of "unmitigated barbarism". "The Tommy Atkins they introduce," wrote Buchanan, "is a drunken, swearing, coarse-minded Hooligan, for whom, nevertheless, our sympathy is eagerly entreated. Yet these pieces were accepted on their publication, not as cruel libel on the British soldier, but as a perfect and splendid representation of the red-coated patriot on whom our national security chiefly depended, and who was spreading abroad in every country the glory of our Imperial flag!"

Eliot to the rescue

Buchanan was astonished that the "contemptible" Barrack-Room Ballads should have been so popular and could explain it only by the fact that even educated readers were in a mood to turn to any writer who could write verse, even doggerel, provided it seemed alive. "They were amused," he went on, "by the free-and-easy rattles, the jog-trot tunes, which had hitherto been heard only in the music halls and read only in the sporting newspapers. In the second place, the spirit abroad today is the spirit of ephemeral journalism, and whatever accords with that spirit – its vulgarity, its flippancy, and its radical unintelligence – is certain to attain tremendous vogue. Anything that demands a moment's thought or a moment's severe attention, anything that is not thoroughly noisy, blatant, cocksure, and self-assertive, is caviare to the man in the street on whom cheap journalism depends, and who ... is often a member of smart society. In the third place, Mr Kipling had the good, or bad, fortune to come at the very moment when the wave of false Imperialism was cresting most strongly upward, and when even the great organs of opinion, organs which, like The Times, subsist entirely on the good or bad passions of the hour, were in sore need of a writer who could express in fairly readable numbers the secret yearnings and sympathies of the baser military and commercial spirit. Mr Kipling, in a word, although not a poet at all, is as near an approach to a poet as can be tolerated by the ephemeral and hasty judgment of the day."

"Political deviation" is a term that is still levelled against Rudyard Kipling even today, making it as difficult as ever for scholars and critics to come to a conclusive decision as to the true measure of his literary achievement. At the end of the First World War the great poet Thomas Stearns Eliot brought the weight of his critical authority to the support of the then undervalued Kipling but even he had to admit to being somewhat puzzled. In a review of *The Years Between* in the *Athenaeum* of May 1919 Eliot wrote: "Mr Kipling is a laureate without laurels. He is a neglected celebrity.... Mr Kipling is not anathema; he is merely not discussed.... There are the many to whom he is a gospel; there are the few to whom he is a shout in the street, or a whisper in the ear of death, unheard. Both are mistaken....

Eliot compared Kipling with Swinburne, both being "men of a few simple ideas" and both "preachers". His is the "poetry of oratory; it is music just as the words of orator or preacher are music." And he continued: "There is one more element in the style or manner of Mr Kipling which demands attention. The eighteenth century was in part cynical and in part sentimental, but it never arrived at complete amalgamation of the two feelings. Whoever makes a study of the sentimentalism of the nineteenth and twentieth centuries will not neglect the peculiar cynical sentiment of Mr Kipling." Eliot concluded: "Mr Kipling is very nearly a great writer. There is an unconsciousness about him which, while it is one of the reasons why he is not an artist, is a kind of salvation. There is an echo of greatness in his naive appeal to so large an audience as he addresses; something which makes him . . . a lonely figure."

Bonamy Dobrée, the critic and literary academic, wrote an article for the *Monthly Criterion* in December 1927 in which he pointed out the impossibility of separating the artist and the politician: "Mr Kipling," he wrote, "cannot be dissociated from the British Empire.... His is no picture of red on the map, since Britannia for him is a goddess. Not only is she a goddess by the fact of her being, but in her nature, for she exacts much toil from her votaries. . . . The Empire then is to be cherished . . . because, like old Rome, it is the most superb instrument to enable man to outface the universe, assert himself against vacancy. Since it unifies the impulses needed to do this, it is Mr Kipling's Catholic Church. . . . Mr Kipling's love of the Empire and his admiration for those virtues it brings out in men, make him apt to find qualities in Englishmen only, which really exist in all races, and this is part of the deformation Mr Kipling the artist has at times undergone at the hands of Mr Kipling the man of action."

Kipling abroad

In general foreign critics have been kinder to Kipling than many of his countrymen. André Maurois, the French novelist and biographer, gave a lecture in 1934, saying: "Kipling's heroic conception of life is not peculiar either to one country or one period. Nearly all men who have fought in wars, who have been leaders . . . have held virtually the same view." Maurois went on to analyse Kipling's characters, pointing out that "there is no place in his world for the man who does

133

not act" but that there is a place for the artist who can also be a man of action in his own sphere. He concluded his paper by asserting: "I dare make a prediction that in a thousand years, or in two thousand years, men will still be reading Kipling and will find him still young."

In Germany, Kipling's works have been widely studied and admired, partly for their ideological affinity with the writings of Nietzsche and the "will to power" theory of human behaviour, partly for their purely literary qualities. Hans Reisiger compared him to Walt Whitman and Georg Engel went even further, suggesting that Kipling had the breadth of vision and narrative power of Homer. George Hermann, writing about the *Jungle Books*, claimed that some of his descriptive passages reminded him of masters of painting such as Michelangelo and Rubens.

In the Soviet Union, Kipling's political message, as might be expected, has had little appeal but some of the books have been highly praised for their stylistic originality. In Italy his books were extremely popular in the early part of the present century and were "rediscovered" after the Second World War, only to go out of favour again in the new political climate of the 1960s.

It is understandable that Kipling's more blatantly patriotic works of prose and poetry should not find an over-enthusiastic response abroad, especially today when colonialism and imperialism are dirty words. Nor can the true verve and spirit of some of his works, especially the verse, be faithfully captured in a foreign language. Thanks to the cinema, however, *The Jungle Book*, even if far removed from the original, remains a children's favourite everywhere.

Editions of Kipling's Works

The following volumes of Kipling's prose works are available in the Centenary Edition published by Macmillan & Co. Ltd. *Actions and Reactions, Animal Stories, Captains Courageous, The Day's Work, Debits and Credits, Diversity of Creatures, The Jungle Book, Just So Stories, Kim, Life's Handicap, The Light that Failed, Limits and Renewals, Many Inventions, Plain Tales from the Hills, Puck of Pook's Hill, Rewards and Fairies, The Second Jungle Book, Soldiers Three, Stalky & Co., Traffic and Discoveries, Under the Deodars, Wee Willie Winkie. Something of Myself* is also published by Macmillan. *Barrack-Room Ballads* are available in an edition published by Methuen, and the *Definitive Edition of Rudyard Kipling's Verse* is published by Hodder and Stoughton.

Picture Acknowledgments

P.1: © 1965 Walt Disney Productions.
P.2: British Museum, London. Photo Freeman.
P.4: Photo Mansell Collection, London.
P.7: Victoria and Albert Museum, London. Photo Freeman.
P.8: Bateman's, Burwash, Sussex. National Trust.
P.9: Victoria and Albert Museum, London. Photo Freeman.
P.10: Bateman's, Burwash, Sussex. National Trust.
P.11: Bateman's, Burwash, Sussex. National Trust.
P.12: left and right, Bateman's, Burwash, Sussex. National Trust; below, photo Governors of Hayleybury and Imperial Service College.
P.13: above, Bateman's, Burwash, Sussex. National Trust; below, Victoria and Albert Museum, London (J. L. Kipling Collection). Photo Freeman.
P.14: left, Bateman's, Burwash, Sussex. National Trust; right, photo Nino Cirani.
P.15: left, Bateman's, Burwash, Sussex. National Trust; right, photo India Office Library, London.
P.16: left, Bateman's, Burwash, Sussex. National Trust; right, photo G. Harper, Brighton.
P.17: National Portrait Gallery, London.
P.18: above, photo Mondadori archives; centre, National Army Museum, London.
P.19: left, British Museum, London. Photo Freeman; right, Radio Times Hulton Picture Library.
P.20: Bateman's, Burwash, Sussex. National Trust.
P.21: above, left and below, Bateman's, Burwash, Sussex. National Trust; above, right, Radio Times Hulton Picture Library.
P.22: Bateman's, Burwash, Sussex. National Trust.
P.23: 1. Bateman's, Burwash, Sussex. National Trust; 2, 3, 4, Radio Times Hulton Picture Library.
P.24: left, Bateman's, Burwash, Sussex. National Trust; right, Radio Times Hulton Picture Library.
Pp.34, 35, 37, 38, 39, 40, 41, 42, 43, 44, 45, 48: photo Freeman.
P.49: Victoria and Albert Museum, London. Photo Freeman.
P.50: Victoria and Albert Museum, London. Photo Freeman.
P.51: British Museum, London.

Pp.52, 53: Victoria and Albert Museum, London. Photo Freeman.
Pp. 54, 55: British Museum, London. Photo Freeman.
P.56: Victoria and Albert Museum, London. Photo Freeman.
P.61: Bateman's, Burwash, Sussex. National Trust.
Pp.64, 69, 74, 80, 82, 87: photo Freeman.
P.88: Mausell Collection, London.
P.90: Mansell Collection, London.
Pp.93, 94, 97, 99, 101, 102, 104: photo Freeman.
Pp.105, 106: Victoria and Albert Museum, London. Photo Freeman.
P.107: Lahore Museum. Photo Scala.
P.108: British Museum, London. Photo Freeman.
P.109: above, Bateman's, Burwash, Sussex. National Trust; below, British Museum, London.
P.110: above, Victoria and Albert Museum, London. Photo Freeman; below, India Office Library, London. Photo R. Z. Fleming.
P.111: Victoria and Albert Museum, London. Photo Freeman.
P.112: Victoria and Albert Museum, London. Photo Freeman.
P.113: Victoria and Albert Museum, London. Photo Freeman.
P.114: British Museum, London. Photo Freeman.
P.115: National Army Museum, London.
P.116: above, India Office Library, London. Photo R. B. Fleming.
Pp.116–17: India Office Library, London. Photo R. B. Fleming.
P.117: above, Victoria and Albert Museum, London. Photo Freeman.
P.118: India Office Library, London. Photo R. B. Fleming.
P.119: India Office Library, London. Photo R. B. Fleming.
P.120: Victoria and Albert Museum, London. Photo Freeman.

The publishers make apology for any inadvertent errors or omissions in the above list of acknowledgments.

1873
/50/

S